# Once Upon a Sign

# Once Upon a Sign

Using American Sign Language to Engage, Entertain, and Teach All Children

Kim Taylor-DiLeva

 LIBRARIES UNLIMITED

AN IMPRINT OF ABC-CLIO, LLC
Santa Barbara, California • Denver, Colorado • Oxford, England

Copyright 2011 by Kim Taylor-DiLeva

**Library of Congress Cataloging-in-Publication Data**

Taylor-DiLeva, Kim.
   Once upon a sign : using American Sign Language to engage, entertain, and teach all children / Kim Taylor-DiLeva.
      pages cm
   Includes bibliographical references and index.
   ISBN 978-1-59884-476-4 (pbk. : acid-free paper) 1. Libraries and the deaf. 2. Libraries and the hearing impaired. 3. American Sign Language--Study and teaching--Activity programs. 4. Children's libraries--Activity programs. I. Title.
   Z711.92.D4T39 2011
   027.6′63--dc22          2010040785

ISBN: 978-1-59884-476-4
EISBN: 978-1-59884-477-1

15 14 13 12 11   1 2 3 4 5

This book is also available on the World Wide Web as an eBook.
Visit www.abc-clio.com for details.

Libraries Unlimited
An Imprint of ABC-CLIO, LLC

ABC-CLIO, LLC
130 Cremona Drive, P.O. Box 1911
Santa Barbara, California 93116-1911

This book is printed on acid-free paper ∞
Manufactured in the United States of America

Photographs throughout book © Stephanie McCauley / iSmile Studio. Used with permission.

# Contents

# Acknowledgments

I would like to thank my parents, Joe and Betty Taylor, and my husband, Nick DiLeva, whose unconditional love, encouragement, and support are always unwavering. Thank you to my children, John and Ava, who make me passionate about what I do and give me the motivation to be a better person every day. Because of you all, my dream of becoming a published author has come true.

# Introduction

Using sign language with hearing children is one of the fastest growing parenting and teaching trends. Parents of babies and toddlers use sign language with their hearing children to improve communication and enhance verbal language, as well as create a strong bond between parent and child. Teachers hope to improve vocabulary knowledge and increase literacy skills and interest in learning. All of these goals are similar to those that librarians wish to achieve in their children's programs.

During storytime and other library programs, books are read in an attempt to enhance the child's verbal language, increase interest in books and learning, increase literacy skills, and more. Parents, teachers, and yes, librarians, have many of the same goals for the children, yet many librarians are not incorporating the use of sign language into their library programs. Some haven't heard much about this growing trend, while others think that they have to be fluent in American Sign Language (ASL) to teach others how to do it, or maybe they are overwhelmed by the thought of learning something completely new. This book will show you that just by incorporating a few signs into your already successful children's programs, you can have a great impact.

Another reason to include sign language in your programs for children and teens is to help hard of hearing or deaf children, or their families, feel more welcome in the library, as well as helping the hearing population be more accepting of others with differences. Your introduction of ASL in your programs will enable children and teens to become more aware of the third-most-used language in the United States.

*Once Upon a Sign: Using American Sign Language to Engage, Entertain, and Teach All Children* is a guide for both public and elementary school librarians who hold programs for infants, toddlers, and their parents; preschool and primary age children; and 'tweens and teens. It will help librarians engage and entertain all children (hearing and hard of hearing) by introducing fun, new, and exciting programs that incorporate ASL signs. Once Upon a Sign may also appeal to early childhood and elementary schoolteachers, who can use the ideas, themes, stories, songs, activities, and signs in this guide to teach concepts and engage their students during read-alouds and other literacy activities.

*Once Upon a Sign* is broken down into four parts for ease of use. Part I is a great introduction to including sign language in your program. It discusses how to get started, how to make your programs more accessible for hard of hearing and deaf children, and the benefits of using sign language with hearing children of all ages. Part II will guide you through a few programs that include sign language that are appropriate for infants and toddlers (ages 0–2) and their parents. You will be able to run a parenting program on baby sign language and be introduced to a few baby storytimes, programs, or "sign and rhyme" times that parents may attend with their babies and toddlers so they can all learn some sign language together. Topics are bathtime, bedtime, and mealtime. Part III will help you integrate sign language into your programs for preschool and primary age children (ages 3–7). Storytime programs for this age group are on friendship, colors, and farm animals. Part IV will guide you through some fun, new programs that you can offer to elementary age children, 'tweens, and teens (ages 8 and up). After reading the book through once and getting ideas for what types of programs you'd like to begin implementing, you can then go back to those specific chapters that will guide you and give you instructions on how to implement the programs in your library or classroom.

Before you can begin to offer sign language programs in your library, it is important for you to understand the many, many benefits of using sign language with hearing babies, toddlers, preschoolers, school-age children, 'tweens, and teens. Let's take a look at those benefits and supporting research studies that show how beneficial sign language can be for hearing children.

## Benefits for Babies and Their Parents

*Helps establish preverbal communication.* Babies and toddlers who cannot yet talk and use their words to communicate can use signs. The muscles in babies' hands develop faster than the muscles in their mouths, allowing them to use their hands to communicate. They naturally learn common gestures like waving good-bye, so it makes sense that giving them some signs to use for common words would give them a way to communicate. Dr. Joseph Garcia, the pioneer in using sign language with hearing babies, states in *Sign with Your Baby: How to Communicate with Infants Before They Can Speak:*

> Visual and muscular coordination are in place much earlier than that—long before vocal skills mature. In other words, your infant has the ability to use their hands to make signs before they can use speech to clearly communicate. Through signing, you will give your infants a way to express themselves that will be more precise and effective than smiling, cooing, and crying. Your young toddlers can use single signs (and many times several signs together) nearly one year before they effectively use speech. (Garcia 2002, 18)

*Promotes verbal learning.* One of the most common questions I am asked is, "Will babies then rely on sign language to communicate and be delayed in their speech?" Not to worry: "Studies conducted at the University of California at Davis by Drs. Linda Acredolo and Susan Goodwyn determined that babies who used symbolic gestures early learned to speak more readily than those babies who did not. Their research also indicated that the signing babies scored higher in intelligence tests, understood more words, had larger vocabularies, and engaged in more sophisticated play" (Garcia 2002, 24). Garcia also states:

> In my observations, the children who used signs in their early language showed above-average understanding of English syntax earlier than those who did not use signs. Children who had not learned signing were just starting to identify objects with words, while the children in our study were already talking about those objects. The signing children had the advantage of previously learning how to identify objects, feelings, and needs through signs. The important thing is that using signs to communicate before speech develops can enhance the overall communication process. (24–25)

*Improves overall communication between parents and babies.* Babies being able to tell you through sign what they want and need eliminates a lot of the guesswork in parenting. When the baby is understood, when you know what he or she wants and needs, it is much less frustrating for both the baby and the parent or caregiver. Without this guesswork and frustration, there is more time for positive interactions with the child (and less "I don't know what you want"). Also, when babies can tell you through sign what they like, what they see on the page of the book, and so on, you can learn more about their interests and likes and what they'd like you to tell them more about. This allows you to expand your conversation around the things they want to learn more about and gives you a view into their minds earlier on. More positive interactions, understanding your child's wants and needs, less frustration, and knowing babies' interests all lead to a much stronger bond between the parent/guardian and the baby.

*Helps babies learn new words through visual aspects.* Sign language signs are often iconic in nature, meaning that the sign often looks like the actual object. For example, for the sign, "house," you draw the roof and walls of a house with your hands. This helps children learn the meaning of new words and therefore helps increase their vocabulary. A larger vocabulary is one of the indicators that preschool teachers look at to show a child's early literacy skills.

*Increases babies' interest level.* When you include sign language while reading a story to a child, it makes the story more interesting and fun, therefore helping to promote a child's interest in books and reading early on, something we, as librarians, all strive for. As Linda L. Ernst states in *Lapsit Services for the Very Young*: "My purpose is to introduce language, literature, and the library to parents and children in a positive fun manner. . . . If you encourage families with very young children to use the library, its materials, and services at the children's earliest stages of being, you will encourage the family to develop into lifelong library users" (1995, 3). Incorporating sign language into your services and storytelling makes your programs more positive and fun, helping to offer everything Ernst described.

## Benefits for Toddlers and Their Parents

*Helps parents understand toddlers' speech.* As speech develops in toddlers, it can sometimes be very difficult to understand what they are saying. They will often say the first sound of a word, like "buh," and the adult is left to try to guess what "buh" means. It could be that they want to play ball, see a bee, want their bottle, or see a butterfly. Anything that starts with the letter B could be the answer, and it is difficult to determine which is correct. When a toddler can use an accompanying sign along with verbal language, he or she can be easily understood. If the child signs ball while saying "buh," the adult can say the word again so that the child hears it said the correct way, also confirming for the child that he or she wants the ball.

*Is engaging and fun!* Just as with babies, using sign language with toddlers has shown increased vocabulary knowledge; interest in books, reading, and learning; and early literacy skills. When toddlers can sign along with a book, they are more involved in the story and therefore more engaged. When they sign along with the adult, they become active participants in the telling of the story and are no longer passive listeners. This makes listening to a story much more fun, interesting, and engaging!

*Involves less frustration for parent and toddler.* Also similar to babies, when toddlers are understood and have successful communication with the help of sign language, they are less frustrated. A less-frustrated toddler means fewer tantrums. (It would be difficult to meet a parent who wouldn't love to have fewer of those!) Also, less-frustrated toddlers who can communicate through sign language may solve their problems with other children better on their own, therefore achieving less biting and hitting, and can understand and identify their emotions more easily. Toddlers feel less frustrated because they are understood. They feel not only understood, but also like they are getting what they want and need, and that they have good communication. All of this helps toddlers feel more secure and sure of themselves—helping to increase their self-esteem.

*Allows quiet discipline from across the room.* An added bonus is that parents can discipline silently when necessary. From across the room (or across the quiet library), parents can give their children a sign like "stop" or "quiet." Parents often find this helpful in quiet places, when they are across the room from their child so that they don't have to yell over a distance, or in uncomfortable situations (like needing to talk about the potty and whether or not the toddler needs to go while in a public place).

## Benefits for Preschool and School-Age Children and 'Tweens/Teens

*Increases interest in learning and books.* Preschool and school-age children, just like babies and toddlers, also show increased knowledge of vocabulary (and sight words in reading) because many sign language signs are iconic in nature; have a higher interest in books and learning; enjoy being involved in the storytelling of the story through sign language; and are more engaged in storytime. In addition, children of these ages show a better understanding of story comprehension and sequence of events in the story when they use the signs to accompany the keywords (the most important words).

*Increases confidence and self-esteem.* Also like babies and toddlers, these children show a higher level of confidence and self-esteem. Dr. Marilyn Daniels has composed and conducted the most research on using sign language in the classroom with preschool and school-age children. In Dancing with Words: Signing for Hearing Children's Literacy, she states, "The parents and caregivers stressed the added excitement about learning they observed in the children and indicated a belief that learning sign language generated increased self-esteem; both of these parental views corroborate the observations expressed by teachers" (2001, 62) She points out what teachers and parents learned about their children using sign language in the classroom and that

> in their remarks the teachers stressed the students' improved academic performance. Of course, this would be expected. However, the teachers did mention that their students acquired more self-confidence and more enthusiasm for learning, as well. The parents also noticed that self-esteem and interest in school had increased since the children were using sign language in their classes. The common area, the advantage that all three (teachers, parents and students) groups were cognizant of, was fun. They all mention that they find an inherent joy in signing. (75)

The children themselves say that adding sign language into learning, reading, and storytime is FUN!

*Makes learning new words easier, using hands and body to make the word.* Sign language is not only a visual language, helping those children who learn better visually, it also allows children to use their bodies and hands to make words. Learning by doing or through movement with the body is called kinesthetic learning. Some children learn best by doing things themselves or using their bodies to show what they mean. Sign language allows these children to create words with their bodies and hands. Because hands are used to show the signs, sign language also helps with fine motor skills and coordination.

*Distinguishes between words that sound the same.* Sign language can help children distinguish between words that are similar or "like" words. For example, with a sign I can show a child the word "which" versus the word "witch" or the word "bat" (the kind that flies) versus the baseball "bat." The two words sound the same, and in the case of the word bat even look the same, and therefore it may be difficult for a child to understand that although the words sound the same, they have very different meanings. Using a sign to show the word and having the iconic nature of that sign helps the child understand the meaning of the word and clarify the difference, therefore helping the child distinguish between the two words.

*Allows easier interaction with special needs children.* Teaching hearing children some sign language not only gives them a head start in the third-most-used language in the United States, it also creates opportunities for those hearing children to interact more easily with the special needs and/or hearing impaired children who sign, live on their street, attend their school, or are in the same classroom.

*Can increase a child's IQ.* Studies conducted by Dr. Linda Acredolo and Dr. Susan Goodwyn demonstrated that children who signed showed an increase in IQ of 8 to 12 points by the time they had reached second grade, versus children who had not signed (Acredolo and Goodwyn 2000).

With all these benefits for hearing children of all ages, it is important that you, as a librarian, in addition to the children's parents and teachers, start to incorporate sign language in your day and programs. As you've just read, sign language helps children learn to love reading and books, have higher literacy skills, have larger vocabularies, and have FUN! There isn't much more you could ask for from a library program that you are offering your young patrons. Also, you'll find very shortly that adding sign language to your library programs will be a lot of fun for you as well.

# Part I

## Introduction to Sign Language Programs in the Library

# Chapter 1

# Getting Started

So now that you know the benefits of using sign language with hearing children, let's look at a few tips to help you get started using it in your library. This chapter also examines how to make your library programs more welcoming and accessible to hard of hearing or deaf children who live in your community.

The first thing you need to do is BREATHE. Sometimes when people start to think about incorporating sign language into their programs or offering some new programs that include sign language, they feel overwhelmed. This book will make it easy and fun by basically holding your hand and taking you step by step through the process of how to either offer a new, fun program or integrate sign language signs into your current program. This is not going to be difficult. In fact, it is going to be FUN!

You are not expected to become fluent in American Sign Language (ASL) to be able to offer these programs or incorporate these ideas. Often you are only required to learn one or two signs and use them. In programs for older children, you may not have to use any signs. It is great if you are interested in and willing to try adding one or two signs to a program and then learning another one or two signs for the next program, and then continue adding to your repertoire. Think of how many signs you would know by next year at this time! Take it easy and slow, and whatever you do, don't become overwhelmed. Pick one or two signs to start with; once you have mastered those, pick another one or two. Learn signs at your own, comfortable pace.

The following chapters explain how to offer a new program, as well as how to start incorporating sign language into your current storytime or lapsit programs. You don't have to demonstrate the ASL signs as a separate part of your program. The key is to just start incorporating it and using it, making it a natural part of your day and your programming.

Know what resources you have at your library and start to make a list of those you want to add. Suggested resources are provided in the back of this book. As you begin incorporating sign language into your programs, people will become more and more interested in sign language and signing with their babies, toddlers, and preschoolers. Parents, 'tweens, and teens will want to look up more information on sign language or to learn more sign language on their own. Know where to point them for the information they seek. Do you have board books or DVDs that parents can use to learn and to teach their babies? Do you have books or suggested Web sites that you can offer to a teenager who wants to learn more sign language? Know your materials and what resources you have available and become aware of what resources you might be missing and need to order for the future. Children and their families will start to ask what you have, so you'll want to be prepared.

Often when you take an ASL course, the manual alphabet is one of the first things you learn. This can be overwhelming to a new person, especially a child. That would mean 26 letters and signs to learn right off the bat. The approach in this book is to use one or two new signs to start with and add more after you know them and are comfortable with them. Words and their accompanying signs will have more meaning to young children than showing them a letter and its manual sign. You want to sign the keywords or the most important words, those they should remember and be able to use after they leave the library program that day. Don't try to demonstrate 26 manual alphabet letters in a 45-minute storytime. What are the chances the children will remember all of them? If you show a handful of signs that are the most important and meaningful keywords supporting your program's theme, there is a better chance they will remember all of them. Be direct, use the important keywords, and use however many you are comfortable with. Starting with one or two is just fine!

You are using sign language to enhance verbal language, not replace it. Almost all of the time you will want to say the word and sign it at the same time. When you choose one or two signs to use with a story you are reading during preschool storytime, have the participants make the sign every time you read the word in the book. When you say "train," participants will sign "train." Every time you say "train," you will sign "train." Saying the word and signing it together will help everyone remember the word and the sign (thereby helping young children learn new vocabulary words.) Therefore, choose the most important keywords that support your theme.

Signing and holding a book may be difficult, because both activities require you to use your hands. There are a few options for addressing this challenge. Choose the one that will help you most depending on the signs you are using. Important factors are whether the signs are one handed or two handed, the age of your participants, and what materials you have in your library. One option is to demonstrate the signs before you read the book. This way you can model how to form each sign the correct way. Then when you are reading the book, you can use one hand as a reminder to your listeners to use the sign. You may then remind them as you read that you are only using one hand because you are holding the book, but that they should use two hands. Another option is to have a helper hold the book for you while you read and sign. This could be a child, a parent, or another library staff member. Yet another option would be to put the book on an easel that is meant to hold books during a read-aloud.

Where a sign is made can influence the meaning of the sign, so when you are learning a new sign you'll want to make sure you are placing your hand in the correct area of your body. A sign made in front of the torso can mean something completely different from a sign made in front of the head. Be sure to show the children where to place their hands to convey the correct meaning of the word.

This also pertains to how a sign is made. Using a wrong finger could change the meaning of the word, so be sure that you are using the correct hand shape as well. Show the program participants how to make the correct hand shape and correct them if necessary. Sometimes it is necessary to show children how to make the correct hand shape by taking their hands and moving their fingers into the correct position. Make sure that you ask permission to take their hands into yours and help them make the correct hand shape.

With babies and toddlers, approximations are okay; they won't always be able to make the signs correctly because their fine motor hand development isn't developed yet. Tell parents that it is okay for them to take their child's hands and form them into the correct hand shape once in a while if the baby will let them (they wouldn't want to do that every time, however). If babies/toddlers are sitting in front of or on the lap of their parents, parents may sign in front of the child or even on the child (instead of on themselves) so that the baby can see the sign and feel where it belongs.

Try to make eye contact with your participants. Babies, toddlers, and autistic children will have trouble with eye contact, and it is fine if they aren't making eye contact with you. They will still learn and participate. You'll also want to make sure that you sit in close proximity to your program participants so that everyone can see. Also be sure to use facial and body expressions, especially to show what a character in a story is feeling and saying with the words.

When you invite everyone to sign along with you, you aren't incorporating sign language signs to put on a performance, but rather to engage and entertain and provide all the benefits that sign language offers hearing children. You want them to sign along with you. If they aren't signing, welcome them to participate in the storytelling of the story through sign, and let them become active participants in your storytime or library program. Give them praise when they sign along with you and when they make the signs in the correct hand shape with proper placement.

One of the wonderful things about integrating sign language programs into your library is that ASL is an actual language. You aren't using made-up or handed down personal hand gestures. You are borrowing signs from an actual language and culture to share the benefits it offers hearing children, and to help engage, entertain, and teach them. Therefore, you'll want to stay as true to the actual language as you can. Look up each sign in a reliable resource and make sure that your hand placement and hand shape are correct. Keep in mind that regional variations of ASL *do* exist, just as different accents exist. An example is that people in the southern United States say the same English words a little differently than people in the northern United States do. The word is the same, but the pronunciation varies. American Sign Language is the same. People who sign in the western part of the United States will sign just a little differently than people in the eastern part of the United States, or than those using ASL in Canada. The signs are slightly different, but they mean the same thing.

You may want to check with agencies in your local area to see if the signs you are making are those used in your region. If not, someone who knows the regional variations for the signs may correct you, and that is fine. As long as you have used a reputable ASL dictionary as a resource to learn your signs, then you are fine using those signs, even if they are slightly different than your region's versions.

Although this book is intended to help you introduce sign language to the hearing population in your library, it is important that you understand ways in which you can help the hearing impaired population who may be attending your programs. If they are not attending because they don't feel understood or welcomed, it may not be because of anything you've done. They may have a more difficult time adjusting to and participating in your regular programs that are offered for the general hearing population. Following are some tips to keep in mind to make your library more accessible to the hearing impaired children in your community:

- *Reduce background noise.* Background noise can make it much more difficult for a hearing impaired person to hear and focus on you and what you are reading or presenting. Check over your storytime room for background noise before your programs. Is there a heating or cooling fan in the room making noise? May it be turned off during your program? Is someone outside the library mowing the library lawn during your program? May they be asked to mow after your program is finished? Is there a clock that ticks loudly? May it be taken out of the room during the program?

- *Use visual aids.* Visual aids can help the hearing impaired participant understand what is being said. Use them whenever and wherever possible.

- *Bring them closer.* Invite hearing impaired participants to sit in close proximity to you and your visuals. If you are reading a picture book, allow them to sit right in front of you so that they can see the pictures clearly. If you are using a projector screen, allow them to sit in the front so they can clearly see what is being presented.

- *Make sure you have their attention.* When you are ready to talk, read, or present, make sure you have the attention of hearing impaired participants. Make sure they are looking directly at you or at the visual aids. If they are looking somewhere else, they are not ready to hear what you have to say. To make sure hearing impaired participants will understand what you are doing, reading, or presenting, be sure that they are paying attention and ready before you speak, read, present, or demonstrate.

- *Use facial and body expressions.* In ASL, facial and body expressions mean almost as much as, if not more than, the signs. If I sign "sad," but look happy, how I look will win out. Facial expressions and body language are important because deaf and hard of hearing people cannot hear the inflection in a voice. If I say no to a toddler, I may say it very softly or very loudly depending on how desperately I mean it. When using ASL signs or conversing with deaf or hearing impaired persons, your expressions will help them understand what you are saying and how it is meant. This is especially important when you are reading a story aloud. Make sure to show in your face and body what the characters are feeling when they say their words—almost to the point of exaggeration. This will help your audience to better understand the story, what the words are, and how the words are meant.

- *Ask yes and no questions.* Throughout your program, ask participants if something happened in the story, etc., to give the hearing impaired children the chance to answer yes or no along with the other participants. This will show you whether they have understood what has happened in your program or storytime. Ask yes and no questions at various times during the program so that you can tell if you should go on or revisit part of the story or concept.

- *Talk to the parents.* Maintain good communication with the parents of the hearing impaired children who are participating in your programs. Let them know that you'll be using visual aids and ask where the best place would be for them to sit. Tell them that they may ask questions or clarify things for their child whenever necessary. Also tell them that if they hear any background noise that may be interfering with their child's ability to comprehend what is happening in the program, they should let you know and you will do your best to minimize it. Keep the lines of communication open and welcoming with the parents of your participants. This will help everyone feel welcome.

- *Use captions.* If you will be showing a film or video, try to get one that is captioned so that your hearing impaired participants can also enjoy the film or video.

- *Use an interpreter when needed.* If you have a program or participant that warrants it, you may want to hire a Certified Sign Language Interpreter to help interpret what is happening in the program.

Almost all of these tips can be very beneficial for the hearing children attending your programs, but they will help your hearing impaired community feel more welcome in your library and as participants in your programs. Following these tips will show that you are respectful and welcoming of their needs and that you want them to be included in your library and programs.

Keeping these tips in minds may be overwhelming at first, but they are meant to make things easier for you. So first, last, and certainly not least, remember to relax and have fun. Sign language is a very fun language, and children take to it fast and easily. Don't feel that it is a stressful, added-on responsibility, or your library patrons and program participants will feel that way as well. You want them to participate and engage in sign language with you. Signing is fun, so present it naturally, and everyone will respond favorably to it. Relax, have fun, and enjoy the ride. Hold my hand and follow the steps provided, and your patrons, from babies on up through parents, will enjoy the ride with you.

The next chapter takes a closer look at how to incorporate sign language into programs for various age groups, starting with infants and toddlers and their parents or caregivers.

# Part II

Programs for Infants, Toddlers, and Their Parents (Ages 0–2)

# Chapter 2

# Working with Infants and Toddlers

Some libraries offer lapsits or toddler storytime classes (which I like to call rhyme and sign storytime) in their libraries, and some don't. Those who don't offer them often don't do so because they don't know what to do in a 30- or 45-minute session to keep babies and toddlers busy and happy. Adding sign language has many benefits—especially for helping babies and toddlers with communication, as discussed in the introduction. Adding sign language to your storytime will also make it more engaging and entertaining for the children (and their parents) who attend, helping to keep the babies and toddlers interested and engaged.

The next few chapters provide examples of popular baby and toddler storytime themes and suggested books, songs, stories, activities, movement, puppets, and more that you can do while integrating sign language into your rhyme and sign time. Which words to sign are shown in italics, and there are pictures of the signs that go along with them.

You will want to start integrating sign language into the themes that you are already doing. Following are some steps that will make adding sign language to any theme you choose much easier.

## 1. Keep It Simple, Simple, Simple!

With babies and sign language, the key is simplicity. Make it easy on yourself and on them by just signing one or two words that repeat in the story. You'll see in the mealtime example in chapter 6 that I have included additional signs for foods that appear in the story, as well as the repeating or frequent keyword. I've added them because you may want to do more signs if you are comfortable doing so (and you can't overwhelm babies and toddlers by doing too many signs, so if you're comfortable you can add in maybe one or two signs per page). I have also added the food signs because parents may ask about them. It is possible that while reading a parent may want to know the sign for a particular food that their baby eats often so that they can use that sign at home.

However, in the bathtime theme you'll notice that I have only signed the most important (and/or repeating) words in the book or in each line of the songs. Children will be able to pick up on sign language much easier if they are just signing a few keywords, not everything. It will also be easier for you to learn and teach when you are just signing a few keywords. Make it simple for you and the babies, toddlers, and their parents by just picking out a few keywords to sign. I stress that I typically recommend starting with just one or two signs. Once you are comfortable (and the babies, toddlers, and parents are comfortable), you may add on some more.

## 2. Say It and Sign It Together!

Words are much easier for babies and toddlers to understand when used in conjunction with sign language. So whereas with older students in the classroom, I will sometimes just sign so that I can get their eye contact and focus, as well as calming and quieting the classroom, I use both signs and words with babies and toddlers.

With babies and toddlers you always want to say and sign the words together. You will find that this makes you slow down a little while speaking, and it will also allow you to repeat yourself a few times while signing. All of this helps babies and toddlers learn new words. So make sure that every time you say those words in the story, you also sign them.

## 3. Don't Overwhelm Yourself!

The examples in the upcoming chapters include many books, songs, and activities, much more than you can possibly use in a 45-minute storytime. This was done so that you may pick and choose the songs you are most comfortable with, the activities you have the materials for, and the books you have at your library, but most important, so that you may choose the books, songs, and activities that use the number of signs you are comfortable with. To start with, choose the books that only have one or two signs along with them, and maybe even a few books that have the same signs used in them. Then choose the songs that have only a few signs, etc. It is easy to look at the various signs and suggested activities and feel overwhelmed. You don't have to learn them all; just pick and choose from the plethora of ideas provided. Learn the few signs that you need for the books and songs you want to do.

Remember, you don't have to learn and become completely fluent in ASL to start using it in your storytime. Start with a few signs, at a pace that you are comfortable with, and then the next time you do that theme, add in a few new signs/stories/songs. Pretty soon you'll be impressed with how many signs you know and can integrate into your storytimes.

## 4. Use Your Resources!

You'll read this again later on in this book—that's how important it is. *Don't forget to use the resources that appear in the back of this book.* For example, the recommended online dictionaries have videos of people making the signs. These make it easy for you to figure out which way the hand should move, or which finger to use to make a particular sign. These resources can help you make sure you are teaching each ASL sign correctly. They are also very helpful for looking up signs you want to use that don't appear in this book. Choose your theme, choose the book you want to use, pick the keywords or repeating words, and look them up in an ASL online dictionary. Learn the signs, and you're ready to go!

## 5. Use Facial Expressions!

Adults usually automatically do this, particularly when they talk to babies. But facial expressions are especially important in sign language. Because deaf and many hard of hearing people cannot hear the inflections in voices (loud or soft, harsh or gentle), they rely on people's faces to tell them. As discussed in the introduction, if I say, "no, no, no" in a playful way to a toddler one time, but yell "no" as he or she reaches for an electrical outlet, the meaning of the word no and the intensity with which I mean it change. It is important when using signs to show the meaning of the word with your face where applicable. Just as in a read-aloud, when there are quotations, we read as if we are actually the person talking to help children understand the meaning. When using an ASL sign, the face helps to show the meaning, so remember to show in your face how the characters feel or how they are saying the words, along with your signs.

## 6. Not Paying Attention—That's Okay!

Sometimes babies' and toddlers' attention wanders. Although in a perfect world, you would have the complete attention of every baby and toddler when conducting a storytime, that just isn't realistic. Babies and toddlers are at the age when they are exploring the world around them. Change up your activities quickly to help re-engage children who have started to explore. Move into a movement activity if they seem antsy, then on to a story activity if they seem ready to sit down and listen. Are they ready to move again? Do an activity with props that allows them to play with items that relate to your theme. In each sample chapter I have provided a suggested, typical 45-minute storytime. You'll notice that there are a book and then a song, a movement activity and then a prop play activity, another book, and then another song. Jump from one kind of activity to the next to ensure that the children are being kept busy, active, and involved in your storytime theme. Adding the signs will naturally help with this, but jumping from one fun thing to the next is a great way to keep babies and toddlers engaged as well

Another thing to keep in mind is that if they are exploring, it doesn't necessarily mean that they are not observing or hearing what is happening in the room. When I teach baby sign language classes, I tell parents that they should keep participating and signing along. If a baby looks up at mom or dad, he or she will see and hear the activity. If a baby looks up at another adult in the room, he or she will still see and hear the activity. Just because babies aren't sitting and watching you doesn't mean they aren't learning and getting the benefits of the storytime. Often parents come to me later on and say, "I didn't think my baby was paying attention, but she signed a word the other day that we've only ever used in class." They pick up on much more than we give them credit for.

## 7. Gestures versus American Sign Language

Remember that you are using signs from another actual language. In essence, you are borrowing from an already established language and culture and using it in your programs. To respect that language, it is important to stay as true to it as you can. If using a sign, don't make up a gesture, but rather use the resources available to you in print and online to look up the actual sign so that you are as accurate as possible. Also, when using and recommending materials to families, look for the words "American Sign Language" or for ASL signs on the books, videos, etc. If you don't see them, the material could contain gestures used to help babies communicate and not actual ASL signs.

I recommend using ASL-based materials as often as possible. The reason is that it is an actual language that can be used when you see a deaf family on the playground, in the grocery store, or living in your neighborhood. Gestures can only be used by the people who know them, which would be very few. American Sign Language can be used with anyone—teachers, interpreters, deaf families, etc.—who knows some ASL. You are more likely to find a preschool teacher who uses ASL signs in his or her class than a preschool teacher who uses made-up gestures. American Sign Language with babies is transferable to real-life application.

## 8. Be Prepared

When you are planning for an upcoming rhyme and sign storytime for your babies and toddlers, select your songs, stories, and activities a few days ahead of time. Practice reading the story and signing together. Practice the songs while signing along. This will help you remember the signs on the day of your storytime, while also making your program flow. You don't want to be checking your cheat sheets while at the same time trying to captivate babies and toddlers. Practicing and being prepared will help you feel comfortable and at ease and will help your patrons enjoy your program much more.

These tips will help you integrate ASL signs easily, comfortably, and accurately into your already established baby and toddler storytimes or a new baby/toddler storytime program. Just remember to start slowly and at the level you are comfortable with. The parents and children will be thrilled if you only teach them one or two signs at first, so start easily and comfortably. Remember that their comfort level will be about the same as yours if you are just getting started. Slow and steady always wins the race!

# Chapter 3

# Baby Sign Language Parent Program

Baby sign language is a fast-growing phenomenon among new parents. Parents are hearing about the great benefits sign language can offer. Since the muscles in babies' hands develop faster than the muscles in their mouths, this allows them to use their hands to communicate. As a result, babies are able to "tell" their parents what they want or need through sign language, helping to reduce the guesswork of parenting and to reduce parent and baby frustration.

Consider offering a program for new parents in your library to help them understand the benefits of signing (especially those benefits that pertain to literacy). This will also allow you to demonstrate to parents how to sign along with stories. You may promote your baby/toddler rhyme and sign storytime, the ASL books in your library, and the board books and picture books that are easy to sign along with (ones that repeat a keyword or two).

Not sure what to say in your parent program? Not to worry. This chapter spells out what to say and do in your baby sign language parent program. First you'll explain the benefits and give the parents some tips for getting started signing with their babies. Next you'll show the parents how to include sign language in their day through stories, songs, playtime, mealtime, etc. Finally, you'll tell parents about the resources available to them—to help them on their baby sign language journey—both those in your library and those they can access online from home. If after reading this chapter you still aren't comfortable with offering a baby sign language class to parents on your own, there are a few organizations (mentioned in the resources section of this book) that have certified baby sign language teachers. Look for one in your area and find out if that person is available to teach the class for you.

Before your program, you'll need to set a date (plan an hour and a half at the most) and get your materials ready. You may want to prepare a list of resources as a handout for the parents listing the books you have available at your library. You will also need a sample story; a song or two; and blocks, various sizes of plastic storage containers, or plastic animals to demonstrate playtime with signing. Promote the program a week or two ahead of time, with flyers or on the library Web site or newsletter, and talk about it to parents who come into the children's room. Following is an outline of the program and suggested songs, stories, and activities to use, as well as a list of resources.

# Introduction/Welcome

Welcome the parents to your library and program, thanking them for attending and letting them know what they will learn. Share the following benefits of using sign language with babies.

## Benefits

Research has shown the following:

- Babies can communicate earlier through sign language (due to the muscle in the hands developing faster than the muscles in the mouth and jaw).

- Signing empowers babies and toddlers to communicate—they gain confidence in their ability to communicate and get their message heard.

- Having better communication through sign language reduces frustration for babies and parents (and their daycare teachers).

- Signing enhances language skills. Parents often ask, "Won't my baby rely on the sign and then not speak?" Let them know that the opposite has been shown to be true in the research and that they should look at baby sign language as a stepping stone. Babies crawl before they learn to walk, but once they start walking they realize that it is easier and faster to get around that way. Sign language for babies is very similar. They can sign before they can talk, but once they start talking they realize that it is easier and faster to be heard and understood.

- Parents may learn what things interest their baby earlier, helping to provide a window into the baby's mind.

- Signing increases the parent and child bond. They understand each other better and feel understood.

- Parents and child-care providers have said that signing is fun and adds an extra element of fun to their day with the baby.

Once the parents understand the benefits of signing with their baby, they'll need to know how to start. Hand out the reproducible "Baby Sign Language: Tips for Getting Started" (p. 17) to each parent. Go over the handout, addressing each point and demonstrating the first few signs to start with. They may take this handout home and refer to it again when they start implementing sign language with their baby.

# Baby Sign Language: Tips for Getting Started

- Use your dominant hand—it doesn't matter if you are right handed or left handed. Use the one you are most comfortable with.

- Don't overwhelm yourself. Start with a few signs and add more as you learn them. Great signs to start with are *milk*, *more*, *eat*, and *all done (finished)*.

**Milk**          **More**          **Eat**          **All Done (Finished)**

- You can't overwhelm babies by doing too many signs at once. So do as many signs as you are comfortable with. Don't use one or two signs and then wait for them to sign back before you use more. They will learn more signs as they watch you. Then when they are ready, they will start signing many signs.

- Babies typically sign back when they are between 8 and 12 months of age. Some sign earlier and some start to sign later. Don't get frustrated if they don't sign back right away. Eventually they will sign back to you, just as every child learns to gesture "bye." Be patient and keep at it. Eventually you'll see the rewards.

- Say the words and sign the sign together every time. We are using sign language to enhance speaking language, not to replace it.

- You may start signing with babies as soon as they can see and are becoming aware of their surroundings and the world around them. It is never too early to start signing, and it is never too late, as the benefits of signing continue through grade school.

- Make eye contact if possible and be in the baby's field of vision.

- Babies will approximate—meaning that their hand shape won't be exactly correct all of the time. That's okay. You should continue to sign the correct way; eventually they will realize that they aren't holding their hands the same as yours and they will correct themselves. Just learn to recognize your baby's versions of the signs so that you can understand what he or she wants or needs.

- There are many different baby sign language programs out there. It is up to you if you want to use a more gestural baby sign system versus ASL signs. Gestural signs also work, but aren't transferrable to everyday use. American Sign Language is an actual language that can be used in child-care centers, in preschools, or with deaf families on the playground, in the grocery store, or on their street.

## Including Sign Language in Your Day—Storytime

You may want to reiterate to parents that signing while reading a story to their child has been shown to help babies learn more new vocabulary words, increase their literacy skills, and increase their interest in books, in addition to helping introduce them to new signs. Choose one to three books to use for demonstration purposes. You may pick any of the book examples in the sample rhyme and sign storytime chapters, or pick one that you know babies and parents enjoy and show them how to sign one or two words that repeat in the story (if they don't know a lot of signs).

Consider the example *Where Is Baby's Mommy* by Karen Katz. It repeats the words "mommy" and "no." You may also choose a popular bedtime story such as *Good Night Moon* by Margaret Wise Brown and sign "good night," or *Time for Bed* by Mem Fox, and sign "bed" and "sleep."

**Katz, Karen.** *Where Is Baby's Mommy?* **New York: Little, Simon, 2001.**

Baby looks around the house trying to find her mommy. This book demonstrates the classic game of hide and seek, with repetition and lift-the-flaps that children adore.

**Signs:** *mommy, no*

**Mommy**

**No**

**Brown, Margaret Wise.** *Goodnight Moon.* **New York: Harper & Row, 1947.**

The classic story tells about a bunny that says goodnight to different objects before going to sleep, which makes for an excellent bedtime story.

**Signs:** *good, night*

**Good**

**Night**

**Fox, Mem.** *Time for Bed.* **New York: Harcourt Brace, 1997.**

The rhymes throughout this story will be appealing to children at bedtime, as Fox writes about different animals as they go to sleep.

**Signs:** *bed, sleep*

**Bed**          **Sleep**

## Including Sign Language in Your Day—Music

Now that you've shown the parents how to sign along with stories, share with them how to sign along with music. Babies and toddlers love music. They love to be sung to when they're very small, and they generally love to sign along when they are listening to music when they get a little bit older.

Music and movement naturally go together. You can't help but start tapping your foot or bobbing your head when you hear a good beat. Therefore, adding sign language signs to the songs you're singing is a natural way to engage your child's body with the song and music. Signing the words of the song will also help babies and toddlers understand the meaning of the song and introduce them to new vocabulary words that they will hear.

There are two ways to add sign language to music. One is to introduce a new song to the child that incorporates sign language. The other is to take a song that parents are already singing and start using sign language signs along with it. For a new song to introduce to parents, use "Pick Me Up!" from *Pick Me Up! Fun Songs for Learning Signs* by Sign2Me. For a song that many parents are already singing to their children, demonstrate the song "Twinkle Twinkle Little Star." Give parents a copy of the reproducible handout (pp. 20–21) so that they can refer to it at home and have a reminder of how to make the signs.

# Fun Songs to Sign with Your Baby

"Pick Me Up!" *Li'L Pick Me Up! Fun Songs for Learning ASL Signs.* Sign2Me /Northlight Communications Inc., 2009. CD.

**Signs:** *up, mommy, more, daddy, food, play, you, today, down, no*

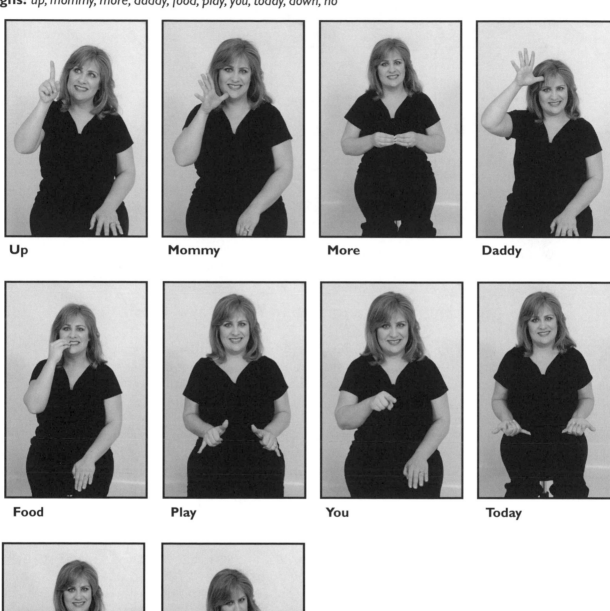

| Up | Mommy | More | Daddy |

| Food | Play | You | Today |

| Down | No |

## Fun Songs to Sign with Your Baby

### Twinkle, Twinkle Little Star

*Twinkle, twinkle* little *star,*
How I *wonder* what you are.
*Up above* the *world* so high,
Like a *diamond* in the *sky.*
*Twinkle, twinkle* little *star,*
How I *wonder* what you are.

**Signs:** *twinkle (shine), star, wonder, up above, world, diamond, sky*

**Twinkle**

**Star**

**Wonder**

**Up Above**

**World**

**Diamond**

**Sky**

## Including Sign Language in Your Day—Playtime and Mealtime

Explain to parents that playtime and mealtime are two other great opportunities in babies' day to teach them some new signs and get them signing back. The times when parents typically have their babies' fullest attention and when they are the most interested are mealtime and playtime. This is when babies are the most alert and interactive, and it therefore gives parents the perfect opportunity to introduce some sign language signs to learn and then use when they want or need a particular item, object, or toy.

Mealtime provides a perfect chance to teach babies signs like *more, all done, water, milk, eat,* and *please* as parents use each word. When parents give their child more food, they should sign (and say) *more*. When giving their child some milk to drink, parents should sign (and say) *milk*.

**Signs:** *more, all done, water, milk, eat, please*

**More**

**All Done**

**Water**

**Milk**

**Eat**

**Please**

Although the signs *more*, *all done*, and/or *please* can often be the first signs that babies use, sometimes babies will first sign a toy or item in the house that is special to them. Also, it is sometimes easier for a baby to understand what an object is, for example, "blocks" versus "more," which is a more abstract concept. It is important to show babies signs for both abstract words and concrete or object words.

Playtime is a fun time to incorporate signs. For this part of your demonstration, you should bring out some playthings and show parents how you would incorporate sign language. Fancy toys are not necessary. For example, you might take out various sizes of plastic storage bowls and lids. Put the bowls inside each other, signing *in* as you do each one. You might then sign *out* as you remove each bowl. You could also stack the tops while signing *on*, and then take the lids off, signing *off*.

**Signs:** *in, out, on, off*

| **In** | **Out** | **On** | **Off** |

You might also want to demonstrate with blocks, a toy that many people already have at home. As you build the blocks up, sign *up*. As babies knock the tower down, sign *down*. Again, you may sign *on* and *off* as you place the blocks on and off.

**Signs:** *up, down, on, off*

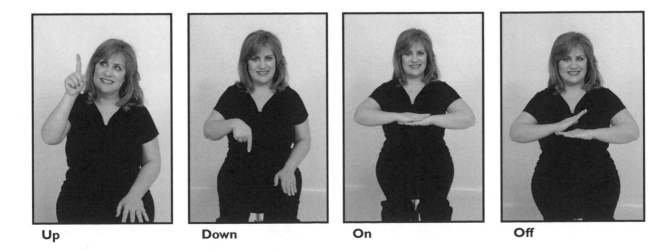

| **Up** | **Down** | **On** | **Off** |

Show parents that they can use signs with anything at home, such as a plastic elephant. Parents could sign *elephant, gray, big, baby, mom, dad*, and any other word that describes the elephant.

**Signs:** *elephant, gray, big, baby, mom, dad*

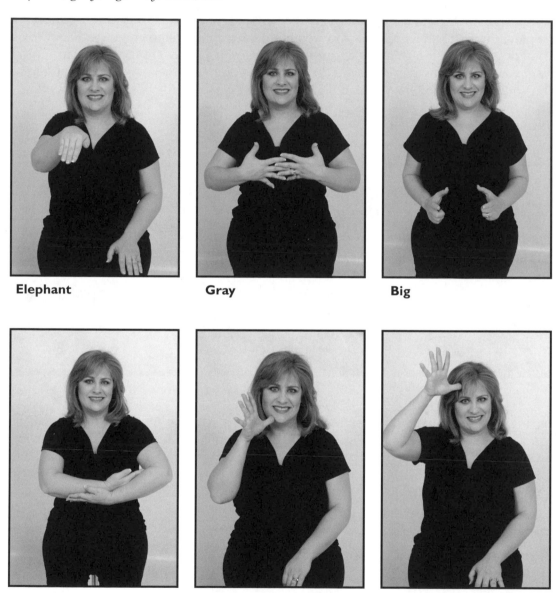

| Elephant | Gray | Big |
| Baby | Mom | Dad |

## Including Sign Language in Babies' Daily Routines

Babies and parents often have daily routines. Take the opportunity to discuss with parents how to incorporate sign language into their daily routines with their babies. Babies and toddlers respond extremely well to routines. They love to know what to expect in their day. Knowing what is coming up next can really help relieve baby/toddler frustration. Demonstrate to parents how they can use signs to show children what is coming up next in their day so that they know what to expect. For example, when it is time for bedtime, they may sign *PJ's, book, song, sleep*. The baby will know that after PJ's are on, then we'll read a book, then sing a song, and then it's time to go to sleep.

**Signs:** *PJ's, book, song, sleep*

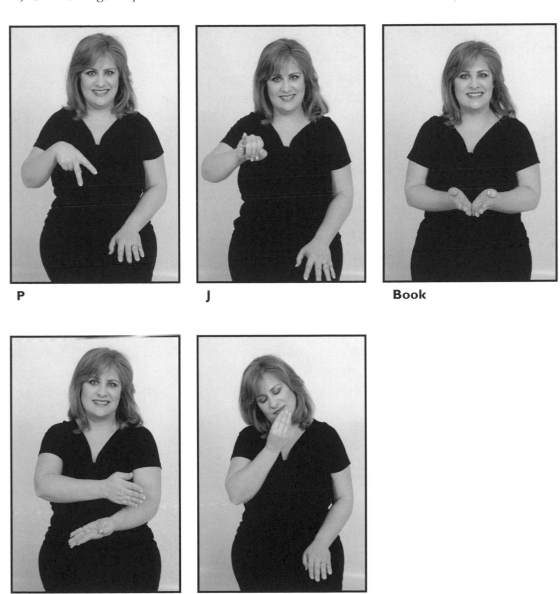

| P | J | Book |

| Song | Sleep |

## Resources

The resources section at the back of this book is another handout to give parents. It includes a list of ASL online dictionaries they can use to look up signs they might want to use with their child. You should also make up your own resources handout listing books and DVDs that are available at your library for parents to borrow. Distribute both of these handouts to parents before they leave.

## Last, But Not Least—Keep Signing

Finally, encourage parents to make signing a regular part of their routine and to keep signing. It is natural to drop signing in the home when a child begins to talk. Children will most likely stop using many signs, and as a result many parents also stop signing. However, there are many, many benefits to continuing to use sign language with children, and it just requires a little effort from the parents to keep signing in the home. Following are the benefits of signing past the baby stage:

- As toddlers are learning to speak, they are often not clear. "Buh" comes out when the toddler means to say ball, balloon, or bug. Having the sign to go along with the "buh" sound can help clarify what the toddler is trying to say, and thus make it possible to say the word correctly back to the child—helping him or her learn the correct way to say the word. This, of course, also helps both with communicating and knowing what exactly it is that the child wants. Is "buh" the balloon the child wants to play with, or is there a bug in the house? The toddler, along with speech, can sign what it is he or she is trying to say.

- Sign language with babies, toddlers, and preschoolers has been shown to increase vocabulary; early literacy skills, better preparing them for learning to read; and their interest in books and learning.

- After using sign language, child-care teachers have reported decreased biting and hitting among signing children, an increased ability to solve problems on their own, and an increased ability to express their feelings.

- For visual and kinesthetic learners (children who learn better by seeing or by creating/doing), learning can be easier and faster when sign language is incorporated. Sign language is a visual language that requires you to move your hands and body to make a word. In addition, many signs (not all, but many) look like the actual object, making it much easier for children to understand the meaning of the word when it is said to them. When signs look like the actual object, they are called iconic.

- Because ASL is an actual language, children may use the signs they know to communicate with deaf children or special needs children in their school, class, street, or community.

## Closing the Program

Offer any handouts that you haven't yet distributed to your participating parents, and perhaps add a flyer about your upcoming programs. Then allow time for questions and answers at the end. If you don't have all the answers to their questions, that is okay. You do, however, have the resources to send them to for the answers.

If you follow the template provided in this chapter, you'll have a very successful program for new parents at your library. They will have learned a lot about how to make themselves and their babies happier through better communication and fun in their home. They will also have learned what other programs and materials you have at your library that they'll want to come back and participate in and/or use.

# Glossary of Signs Used in Baby Sign Language Parent Program

**All Done (Finished)**

**Baby**

**Bed**

**Big**

**Book**

**Dad (Daddy)**

**Diamond**

**Down**

**Eat, Food**

**Elephant**

**Good**

**Gray**

# Glossary of Signs Used in Baby Sign Language Parent Program

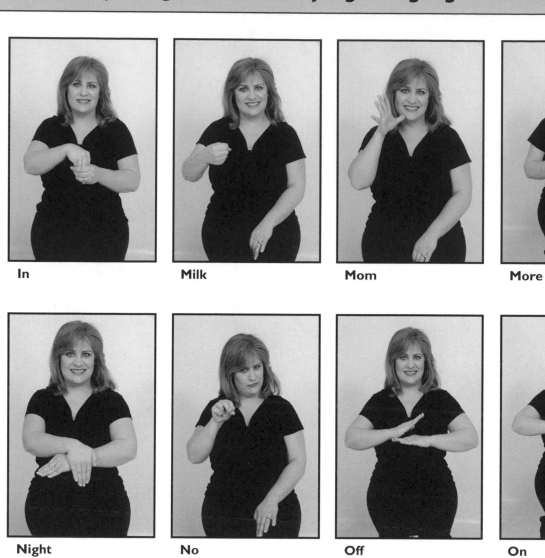

**In**

**Milk**

**Mom**

**More**

**Night**

**No**

**Off**

**On**

**Out**

**P**

**J**

**Please**

# Glossary of Signs Used in Baby Sign Language Parent Program

**Sky**

**Sleep**

**Song**

**Star**

**Today**

**Twinkle**

**Up**

**Up Above**

**Water**

**Wonder**

**World**

**You**

# Chapter 4

# Bath and Body—Rhyme and Sign for Babies/Toddlers

> **Signing Tip**: Babies can sign before they can speak. Teaching babies signs for their everyday activities can greatly increase their communication. Babies and toddlers will be able to communicate whether or not they want to take a bath or have more bubbles, balls, duckies, or water. They can also let you know if the water is too hot or cold.

Babies and toddlers generally love bathtime. It is a great opportunity to have some fun playing in the water, so a theme on bathtime would be great to incorporate into your lapsit/toddler time. Children will love to learn the signs as they get the opportunity to play with bubbles; pretend to wash their bodies; and go through books, songs, games, and activities. This chapter introduces ideas to enhance your already established lapsit/toddler theme on bathtime or help you create one. It includes books, songs, movement, crafts, and other activities that can be fun for children and their parents to participate in.

## Sample Lesson Plan for a 45-Minute Lesson

Following is a suggested lesson plan for a 45-minute rhyme and sign storytime using the bathtime theme. You may vary this plan based on the materials you have in your library, the songs you are comfortable singing, and the materials you have available for craft time. Many book, song, activity, and craft ideas have been supplied in this chapter. The key is making your lesson plan one that you are comfortable with.

*Welcome Song—"Hello Friends"*

*Books—Bathtime for Biscuit by Alyssa Satin Capucilli*

*Song—"Where Is Baby's Tummy?"*

*Movement—Wash Our Heads, Shoulders, Knees, and Toes*

*Book—Scrubba Dub*

*Activity—Bubbles*

*Movement—Washing Hokey Pokey*

*Closing Song—"The More We Sign Together"*

*Activity—Water Play*

*Craft—Washcloth Bunnies*

*Closing Song—"Good-bye Friends"*

## Welcome Song

Signed words are shown in italics for the song and illustrated below.

### "Hello Friends" (Sing to the tune of "Goodnight Ladies.")

*Hello friends, hello friends, hello friends,* we're *glad* you're here *today.*
*Hello* [each child in the class gets a turn with his or her name here], we're *glad* you're here *today.*
*Hello everyone, hello everyone, hello everyone,* we're *glad* you're here *today.*

**Signs:** *hello, friends, glad, today*

| **Hello** | **Friends** | **Glad/Happy** | **Today** |

## Theme

Introduce the theme of the day—bathtime. During this segment, discuss bathtime and introduce a few words and signs that go along with the theme.

## Stories

Read a few of the following stories with signs, and use some of the others for a bathtime display.

**Capucilli, Alyssa Satin.** *Bathtime for Biscuit.* **New York: HarperCollins, 1998.**

Biscuit is a dog whose owner struggles to give him a bath. After Biscuit and another dog have played and gotten themselves dirty, they both take a bath.

**Signs:** *bath*

**Bath**

**DeFelice, Cynthia.** *Casey in the Bath.* **New York: Farrar, Straus & Giroux, 1996.**

In this story, Casey hates taking baths, but when he gets a magical soap, this all changes. He then has fun in the tub and loves to take baths.

**Signs:** *bubbles, soap*

**Bubbles**

**Soap**

**Goodman, Joan.** *Bernard's Bath.* **Honesdale, PA: Boyds Mills Press, 1996.**

Bernard is an elephant who hates taking baths. Once he sees others do it, he sees what fun it can be and learns to love it. Children will be able to see that baths can be fun as well.

**Signs:** *bath*

**Optional sign:** *no*

**Bubbles**

**Water**

**Jarman, Julia.** *Big Red Tub.* **New York: Orchard Books, 2004.**

Stan and Stella have fun in their big red tub, but once all the animals join in, their tub takes them on an adventure.

**Signs:** *bubbles, water*

**Optional:** Pretend to splash the water with your hands when you read the word splash.

**Bath**

**No**

**Johnson, Jane.** *Little Bunny's Bathtime.* **Wilton, CT: Tiger Tales, 2004.**

Little bunny does not want to share a bath with his brothers and sisters. Once he sees how much fun they had, he decides he wants to take a bath. He takes one by himself, which also gives him all the attention from his mom.

**Signs:** *bath, wash, clean, water, soap, dirty*

**Bath**

**Wash**

**Clean**

**Water**

**Soap**

**Dirty**

**Krensky, Stephen.** *Bubble Trouble.* **New York: Aladdin Paperbacks, 2004.**

In this story, bubbles start to float out of the tub and out the door, creating trouble and a fun read for children.

**Signs:** *bubbles*

**Bubbles**

**Mayer, Gina, and Mercer Mayer.** *Just Me in the Tub.* **Racine, WI: Western Publishing, 1994.**

Little critter enjoys a bubble bath and toys when it's time to wash up. This story will help show children that baths can be fun, especially when little critter is dry and clean afterward.

**Signs:** *water, wash*

**Optional signs:** *bath, bubble, pajamas (PJ's), tub (T-U-B), cold, dry*

**Water**     **Wash**     **Bath**     **Bubbles**

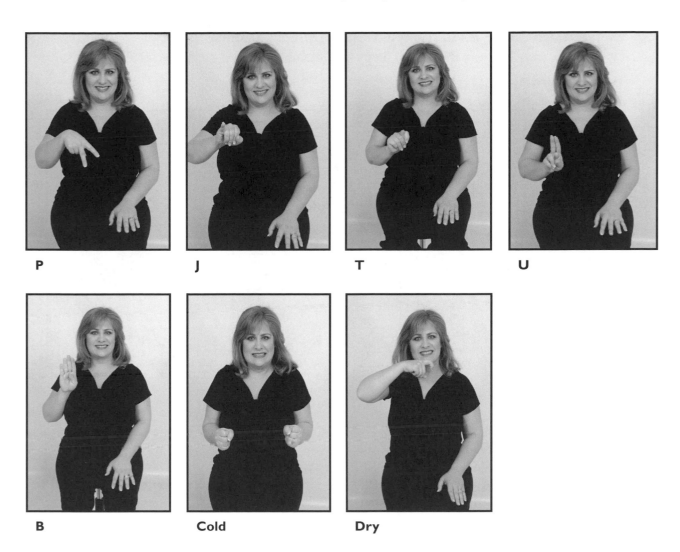

P  J  T  U

B  Cold  Dry

**Philip, Neil.** *The Fish Is Me: Bathtime Rhymes.* **New York: Clarion Books, 2002.**

This book is a collection of songs about bathtime. Choose the songs you think your lapsit group would most like and sign the most-used words in those songs. (See the glossary at the end of this chapter for signs to choose from.)

**Van Lann, Nancy.** *Scrubba Dub.* **New York: Atheneum Books for Young Readers, 2003.**

The rhymes in this story will make this a fun book to read. Children can follow along as a bunny who has gotten himself dirty cleans up by taking a bath.

**Signs:** *wash*

**Optional sign:** *bubbles*

Wash  Bubbles

**Ziefert, Harriet.** *Harry's Bath.* **New York: Sterling Publishing, 2004.**
In this book, Harry the hippo plays in the bathtub while he cleans up.

**Signs:** *tub*

T                                    U                                    B

## Songs

Italicized words should be signed.

**"Where Is Baby's Tummy?" In** *Li'L Pick Me Up! Fun Songs for Learning ASL Signs.*
**Sign2Me/Northlight Communications, 2009. CD.**
Sign the word *where* every time it is said in the song. You may also have the parents and
caregivers point to the baby's tummy, nose, mouth, and toes when the song says, "It's
right there," showing baby where each body part actually is.

**Signs:** *where*

**Where**

de Azevedo Coleman, Rachel. "I Wash My Hands." In *Baby Signing Time! Vol. 2 Music CD*. Two Little Hands Productions, 2007.

> **Signs:** *wash, soap, water*

| **Wash** | **Soap** | **Water** |

"The Bubble Song." *Everything Preschool.* http://www.everythingpreschool.com/themes/bubbles/songs.htm. Accessed April 29, 2010.

> Sung to the tune of "Ten Little Indians," this song will get children counting, signing, and popping those bubbles.

> **Signs:** *bubbles*

**Bubbles**

### "My Bubbles Flew Over the Bathtub"
### (Sing to the tune of "My Bonnie Lies Over the Ocean.")

My *bubbles* flew over the water,
My *bubbles* flew over the tub,
My *bubbles* flew out of the bathroom,
Please *come back* my *bubbles* and scrub.

*Come back*, *come back*, oh *come back* my *bubbles* and scrub-a-dub.
*Come back*, *come back*, oh *come back* my *bubbles* and scrub.

**Signs:** *bubbles, come back*

**Bubbles**            **Come Back**

### "C-L-E-A-N" (Sing to the tune of "B-I-N-G-O.")

There was a child all full of *dirt*.
She needed to get *clean*.
C-L-E-A-N
C-L-E-A-N
C-L-E-A-N
She needed to get *clean*.

Repeat the phrase again and put a clap in for the N in clean.
Repeat the phrase again and put a clap in for the A and N in clean, etc., until you are clapping all of the letters.

**Signs:** *dirt(y)*, *clean*

**Dirt(y)**                    **Clean**

## Movement

Italicized words should be signed.

### "Clap Your Hands"

Clap your hands, 1, 2, 3
Clap your hands, just like me.
Roll your hands, 1, 2, 3,
Roll your hands, just like me.

Continue with stomp your feet, roll your feet, circle your leg, circle your other leg, circle your arm, circle your other arm, rub your belly, roll your shoulders, circle your head, and then end with clap your hands again.

### "Head to Toe"

*Wash* fast, then *wash* slow.
Let's *wash* our bodies from head to toe.
*Wash* your hair fast, then *wash* slow.
Let's *wash* our bodies from head to toe.
*Wash* your face fast, then *wash* slow.
Let's *wash* our bodies from head to toe.

Continue washing the parts of the body, working your way down from head to toe.

**Signs:** *wash*

**Wash**

## "This Is The Way We Wash Our Hands"
### (Sing to the tune of "Here We Go 'Round the Mulberry Bush.")

This is the way we *wash* our toes, *wash* our toes, *wash* our toes,

This is the way we *wash* our toes, at bathtime in the morning.

This is the way we *wash* our legs, *wash* our legs, *wash* our legs,

This is the way we *wash* our legs, at bathtime in the morning.

Continue washing the parts of the body, working your way up from toes to hair.

**Signs:** *wash*

**Optional sign:** *bath*

**Wash**

**Bath**

## "Washing Hokey Pokey" (Sing to the tune of "Hokey Pokey.")

You put your right foot in, you take your right foot out.

You put your right foot in, and you *wash* it all about.

You do the hokey pokey and you get yourself real *clean*.

That's what it's all about.


You put your left foot in, you take your left foot out.

You put your left foot in, and you *wash* it all about.

You do the hokey pokey and you get yourself real *clean*.

That's what it's all about.

Act out the "Hokey Pokey" just as you regularly would, adding in the washing (and the signing, of course.) Continue washing all of the different parts of the body and then put your whole self in.

**Signs:** *wash, clean*

**Wash**  **Clean**

"Wash Our Head, Shoulders, Knees, and Toes"
(Sing to the tune of "Head, Shoulders, Knees, and Toes.")

We *wash* our head, shoulders, knees and toes, knees and toes,

We *wash* our head, shoulders, knees and toes, knees and toes,

We *wash* our eyes and ears and mouth and nose.

We *wash* our head, shoulders, knees and toes, knees and toes.

Point or wash each body part as you say each body part.

**Signs:** *wash*

**Wash**

## Puppets

If you want to add puppets to this storytime, use the movement songs above—"Head to Toe" and/or "This Is the Way We Wash Our Hands"—and wash the body parts of a stuffed animal or puppet.

## Activities/Games/Props

### Water Play

Fill up some tubs or buckets with water, put them outdoors on the grass, and let the children play with rubber duckies, boats, and other water toys in the water. (If you choose this activity you might want to ask the parents ahead of time to bring in an extra set of clothing to change their children into when they're done. This is a great activity to put at the end of storytime on a nice day and have water play outside.)

**Signs:** *water*

**Water**

**Bubbles**

Blow bubbles and let the children pop them.

**Signs:** *bubbles*

**Bubbles**

**Dolly Bathtime**

Bring in baby dolls and let the children give their dollies a bath using real sponges. They can wash them using the "Head to Toe" or "This Is the Way We Wash Our Hands" songs in the movement section.

**Bath Toy Time**

Dump out a bunch of bath toys and let the children play with them. You may show them the signs for the various items they are playing with like ducks, boats, crabs, etc.

# Crafts

**Handprint Bathtub**

**Materials Needed:** Large white mural paper, blue paint, bathtub template (see the appendix)

**Directions:** Draw a large outline of a bathtub on your mural paper. Have parents stick their babies' or toddlers' hands in the paint and then inside the tub on the mural to make the water inside the tub.

**Bubbles Everywhere**

**Materials Needed:** coloring page with a bathtub on it (see the template in the appendix), bubble stickers or foam bubbles

**Directions:** Give each child a coloring sheet and let the children put the stickers or foam bubbles spilling over the bathtub.

**Washcloth Bunnies**

**Materials Needed:** washcloth, clear rubber bands, ribbon, wiggle eyes, pom-poms, double-sided sticky tape (in place of glue), and parent help.

**Directions:** Give each child a washcloth and fold it in half to make a triangle. Roll the cloth from the small point out to the long side. Bend the washcloth in half and then in half again. Put a rubber band one to two inches up from the bent end, to make the bunny ears stand up. Wrap ribbon around the bunny (hiding the rubber band.) Let the babies and toddlers put on the wiggle eyes and pom-pom noses with their sticky tape.

**Washcloth Bunny**

## Closing Song

Italicized words should be signed.

"The More We Sign Together"
(Sing to the tune of "The More We Get Together.")

The *more* we *sign together, together, together,*
The *more* we *sign together,* the *happier* we'll be.
For *your friends* are *my friends* and *my friends* are *your friends,*
The *more* we *sign together* the *happier* we'll be.

**Signs:** *more, sign, together, happy, your, friends, my*

**More**

**Sign**

**Together**

**Happy**

**Your**

**Friends**

**My**

### "Good-bye Friends" (Sing to the tune of "Goodnight Ladies.")

*Good-bye friends, Good-bye friends, Good-bye friends,* we'll *see you* here *again.*

*Good-bye* [each child in the class gets a turn with his or her name here], we'll *see you* here *again.*

*Good-bye everyone, Good-bye everyone, Good-bye everyone,* we'll *see you* here *again.*

**Signs:** *good-bye, friends, see you, again*

**Good-bye**

**Friends**

**See You**

**Again**

Bathtime can be a real joy for children. Not necessarily because they're happy about getting clean, but because of the water, bubbles, and all the great water toys. Learning some signs to use for the things they enjoy can make bathtime much more enjoyable and fun for babies and toddlers. The next chapter includes a rhyme and sign storytime using the theme bedtime.

# Glossary of Signs Used in Bath and Body Theme

**Again**

**Bath**

**Bathroom**

**Bubble(s)**

**Clean**

**Cold**

**Come Back**

**Dirty**

**Dry**

**Duck/Ducky**

**Friends**

**Glad/Happy**

# Glossary of Signs Used in Bath and Body Theme

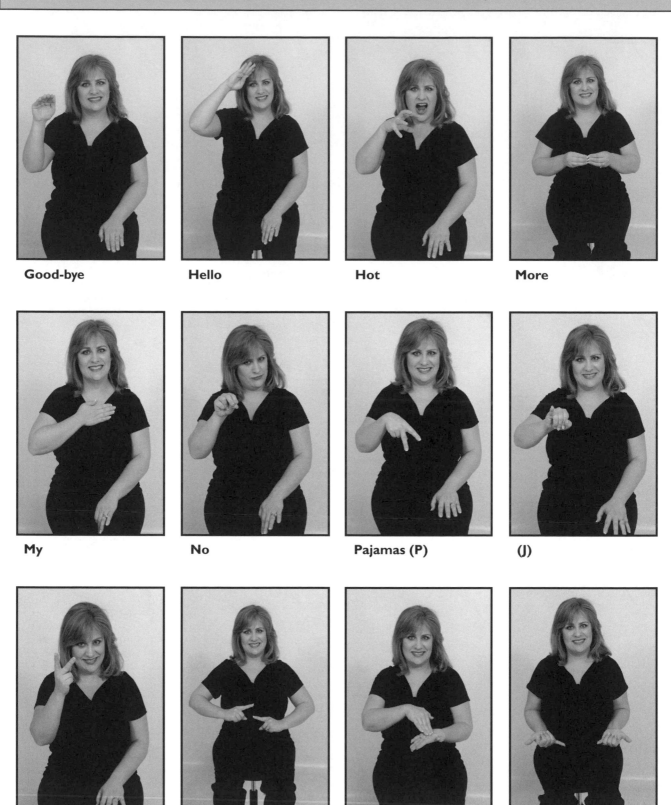

Good-bye

Hello

Hot

More

My

No

Pajamas (P)

(J)

See You

Sign

Soap

Today

# Glossary of Signs Used in Bath and Body Theme

**Together**

**Tub  (T)**

**(U)**

**(B)**

**Warm**

**Wash**

**Washcloth**

**Water**

**Wet**

**Your**

# Chapter 5

# Bedtime—Sample Rhyme and Sign for Babies/Toddlers

> **Signing Tip**: Babies and toddlers respond extremely well to routines. They love to know what to expect in their day. Knowing what is coming up next can really help relieve baby/toddler frustration. Use signs to show the children what is coming up next in their day so that they know what to expect. For example, when it is time for bedtime, sign *PJs*, *book*, *song*, *sleep*. Baby will know that after PJs are on, then we'll read a book, then sing a song, and then it's time to go to sleep. Pretty soon, they may sign to you what is coming up next in the bedtime routine.

Even though babies and toddlers would love to stay awake and not miss out on anything, bedtime/naptime is a very important part of their day. Settling down, reading a story, singing a lullaby, and more are enjoyed by young children. Adding signs is natural for an extra element of fun and enjoyment by both adults and children. Children in your storytime will love to learn the signs as they get the opportunity to use them with books, songs, games, and activities.

This chapter introduces ideas that may be used to enhance your already established lapsit/toddler time. It includes books, songs, movement, crafts, and other activities that are fun for children to participate in.

## Sample Lesson Plan for a 45-Minute Lesson

Again, feel free to modify and replace these resources with other books, songs, or activities that you have in your library and/or are most comfortable using.

*Welcome Song—"Hello Friends"*

*Book—Time for Bed by Mem Fox*

*Song—"Twinkle, Twinkle Little Star"*

*Movement—Teddy Bear, Teddy Bear Turn Around by Penny Dann*

*Book—Goodnight Moon by Margaret Wise Brown*

*Activity—Peek-a-Boo*

*Puppets—Teddy Bear Dance*

*Closing Song—"The More We Sign Together"*

*Activity—Flashlight Tag*

*Craft—Find the Stars and Moons*

*Closing Song—"Good-bye Friends"*

## Welcome Song

Signed words are shown in italics for the song and illustrated below.

### "Hello Friends" (Sing to the tune of "Goodnight Ladies.")

*Hello friends, hello friends, hello friends,* we're *glad* you're here *today.*
*Hello* [each child in the class gets a turn with his or her name here], we're *glad* you're here *today.*
Hello everyone, *hello everyone, hello everyone,* we're *glad* you're here *today.*

**Signs:** *hello, friends, glad, today*

| **Hello** | **Friends** | **Glad/Happy** | **Today** |

## Theme

Introduce the theme of the day—bedtime. You may want to begin your storytime by talking about bedtime and the words/signs for the things they'll see at bedtime.

## Stories

**Boynton, Sandra.** *The Going to Bed Book.* **New York: Little, Simon, 1982.**

In this book, animals prepare for bed by doing things such as taking a bath and brushing their teeth. Children will enjoy the silly nature of this book before bedtime.

**Signs:** *bath, pajamas (PJ's), brush teeth, moon, bed, good night, lights off, sleep*

**Bath**          **P**          **J**          **Brush Teeth**

**Moon**          **Bed**          **Good**          **Night**

**Lights Off**          **Sleep**

**Boynton, Sandra.** *Night-Night Little Pookie.* **New York: Robin Corey Books, 2009.**
 The rhymes in this book will be a great bedtime story as children see Pookie's mom put him to bed.

**Signs:** *pajamas (PJ's), bed, brush, wash, blanket, lights off, kiss, love, good night*

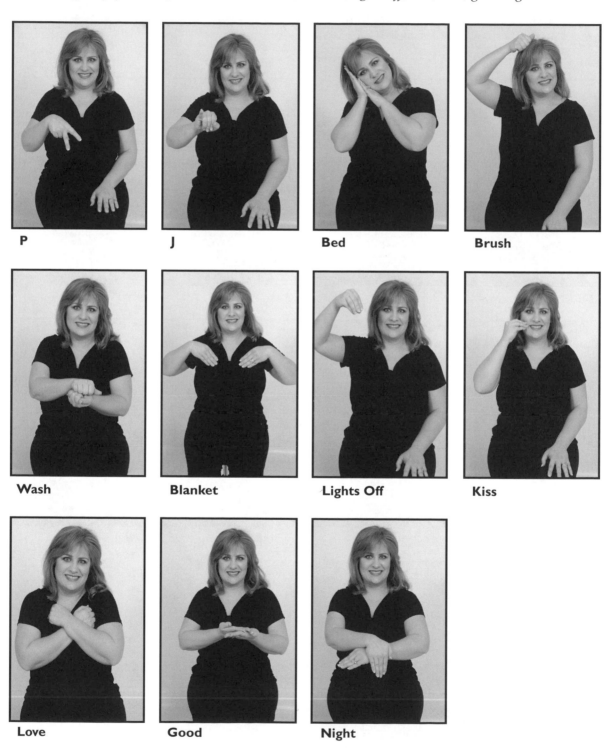

| | | | |
|---|---|---|---|
| **P** | **J** | **Bed** | **Brush** |
| **Wash** | **Blanket** | **Lights Off** | **Kiss** |
| **Love** | **Good** | **Night** | |

**Brown, Margaret Wise.** *Goodnight Moon.* **New York: Harper & Row, 1947.**

The classic story tells about a bunny who says goodnight to different objects before going to sleep, which makes for an excellent bedtime story.

**Signs:** *good, night*

**Good**       **Night**

**Fleming, Denise.** *Time to Sleep.* **New York: Henry Holt, 1997.**

All of the hibernating animals realize that winter is upon them and it is time to go to sleep.

**Signs:** *winter, sleep*

**Winter**       **Sleep**

Fox, Mem. *Time for Bed*. New York: Harcourt Brace, 1997.

The rhymes throughout this story will be appealing to children at bedtime, as Fox writes about various animals as they go to sleep.

**Signs:** *bed, sleep*

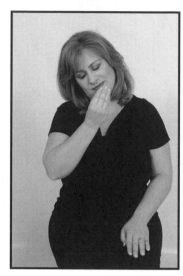

**Bed**        **Sleep**

Lloyd-Jones, Sally. *Time to Say Goodnight*. New York: HarperCollins, 2006.

In this story, various types of animals put their babies to sleep at night. It ends with a young boy falling asleep on a bed filled with the stuffed animals.

**Signs:** *close your eyes, sleep*

**Close Eyes**        **Sleep**

**McBratney, Sam.** *Guess How Much I Love You.* **Somerville, MA: Candlewick Press, 1994.**
Find out how much Little Nutbrown Hare and Big Nutbrown Hare love each other in this story.

**Signs:** *I love you, love*

**I Love You**

**Love**

**Nakamura, Katie Riley.** *Song of Night.* **New York: Blue Sky Press, 2002.**
This book follows various animals and their bedtime rituals.

**Signs:** *bath, brush teeth, song, book, lights out, moon, dreams, close eyes, sleep, kiss, I love you*

**Bath**

**Brush Teeth**

**Song**

**Book**

**Lights Out**

**Moon**

**Dreams**

**Close Eyes**

**Sleep**

**Kiss**

**I Love You**

**Rathman, Peggy.** *10 Minutes till Bedtime.* **New York: G.P. Putnam's Sons, 1998.**

Read along and follow a young boy as he counts down the 10 minutes he has left until bedtime.

**Signs:** *bed*

**Bed**

**Robbins, Maria Polushkin.** *Mother, Mother, I Want Another*. **New York: Dragonfly Books, 1978.**

> Mrs. Mouse asks her friends for help when she thinks baby mouse is asking for another mother, but he actually wants another goodnight kiss.

**Signs:** *mother, kiss*

**Mother**             **Kiss**

**Root, Phyllis.** *Ten Sleepy Sheep*. **London: Walker Books, 2004.**

> The sheep in this story are reluctant to go to bed, but once they find a comfortable place to rest, they fall asleep.

**Signs:** *sleep*

**Optional signs:** *numbers 1–10*

**Sleep**             **One**             **Two**             **Three**

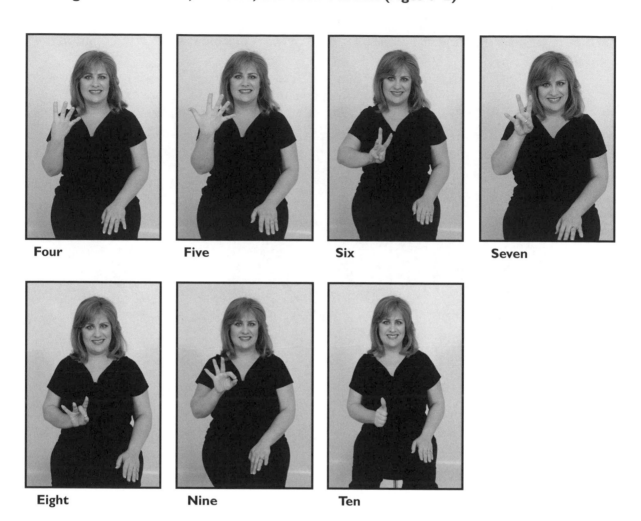

Four        Five        Six        Seven

Eight        Nine        Ten

**Willems, Mo.** *Don't Let the Pigeon Stay Up Late.* **New York: Hyperion, 2006.**

In this story, your child will have fun reading about the pigeon who denies he is tired and keeps making excuses, until he finally falls asleep.

**Signs:** *tired*

**Optional sign:** *good night*

Tired        Good        Night

## Songs

The italicized words should be signed.

**"Sleepy Time Is Near." In** *Li'L Pick Me Up! Fun Songs for Learning ASL Signs.* **CD. Sign2Me/Northlight Communications Inc., 2009.**

**Signs:** *where, pillow, bed, blanket, close eyes, music, hug, dreams*

**Where**

**Pillow**

**Bed**

**Blanket**

**Close Eyes**

**Music**

**Hug**

**Dreams**

de Azevedo Coleman, Rachel. "The Sleep Song." In *Baby Signing Time! Vol. 2 Music CD.* Two Little Hands Productions, 2007.

**Signs:** *sleep, bath, pajamas, brush teeth, book*

**Sleep**　　　　**Bath**　　　　**P**

**J**　　　　**Brush Teeth**　　　　**Book**

"Twinkle, Twinkle Little Star"

Twinkle, twinkle little *star*,
How I *wonder* what you are.
*Up above* the *world* so high,
Like a *diamond* in the *sky*.
Twinkle, twinkle little *star*,
How I *wonder* what you are.

**Signs:** *twinkle (shine), star, wonder, up above, world, diamond, sky*

Twinkle          Star          Wonder          Up Above

World          Diamond          Sky

de Azevedo Coleman, Rachel. "Starry Night." In *Baby Signing Time! Vol. 3, A New Day Music CD.* Two Little Hands Productions, 2008.

**Signs:** *moon, star*

Moon          Star

de Azevedo Coleman, Rachel. "Night Time Is the Right Time." In *Baby Signing Time!* *Vol. 3, A New Day Music CD.* Two Little Hands Productions, 2008.

**Signs:** *story, day, hug, bed, close your eyes, good night*

| Story | Day | Hug | Bed |

Close Eyes     Good     Night

de Azevedo Coleman, Rachel. "Night Time Comes." In *Good Night Baby: A Collection of Lullabies Music CD.* Two Little Hands Productions, 2006.

**Signs:** *night, sleep*

Night          Sleep

## "Five Little Children Jumping on the Bed"

*Five* little children jumping on the *bed*,
One fell off and *bumped* his head [sign *hurt*].
*Momma* called the doctor and the doctor said.
"*No* more children jumping on the *bed*.

*Four* little children jumping on the *bed*
One fell off and *bumped* her head [sign *hurt*].
*Momma* called the doctor and the doctor said,
"*No* more children jumping on the *bed*

*Three* little children jumping on the *bed*,
One fell off and *bumped* his head [sign *hurt*].
*Momma* called the doctor and the doctor said,
"*No* more children jumping on the *bed*."

*Two* little children jumping on the *bed*,
One fell off and *bumped* her head [sign *hurt*].
*Momma* called the doctor and the doctor said,
"*No* more children jumping on the *bed*."

*One* little child jumping on the *bed*,
She fell off and *bumped* her head [sign *hurt*].
*Momma* called the doctor and the doctor said,
"*No* more children jumping on the *bed*."

**Signs:** *five, four, three, two, one, bed, hurt, mom, no*

**Five**

**Four**

**Three**

**Two**

**One**

**Bed**

**Hurt**

**Mom**

**No**

### "Rock-a-Bye Baby"

Rock-a-bye *baby* on the tree top.

When the *wind* blows the cradle will rock.

When the bough *breaks* the cradle will *fall*,

And down will come *baby* cradle and all.

**Signs:** *baby, wind, break, fall*

**Baby**

**Wind**

**Break**

**Fall**

## "Diddle, Diddle Dumpling"

Diddle, diddle, dumpling, my son John,

Went to *bed* with his trousers on;

One shoe off, and one shoe on,

Diddle, diddle, dumpling, my son John!

Go around the room singing this song for each child in your lapsit. Substitute the name John with each child's name and substitute daughter in the place of the word son (and hers instead of his) if singing to a girl in the class.

**Signs:** *bed*

**Bed**

## Movement

**Cousins, Lucy.** *Wee Willie Winkie and Other Nursery Rhymes.* **New York: Dutton Children's Books, 1997.**

Children may act out this rhyme as if they are Wee Willie Winkie.

**Signs:** *bed*

**Bed**

**Dann, Penny.** *Teddy Bear, Teddy Bear Turn Around.* **Hauppauge, NY: Barron's Educational Series, 2001.**

Use the book for your reference as you, along with the parents and children, act out the movements while you sign the word bear.

**Signs:** *Bear*

**Bear**

## Puppets

### Teddy Bear Dance

If you want to do this puppet activity, but don't have enough teddy bears for each child, you may want to ask parents to bring a teddy from home for the next storytime. Have the babies/toddlers hold a teddy bear and follow the actions with their teddy bears.

Hold your teddy bear,
Squeeze him tight.
Hold him left and hold him right.
Hold him up and hold him down,
Then dance with him all around.
Hold him front and hold him back,
Pretend he's crawling up your back.
Where'd he go? He's hiding, see.
Oh, I've got him right next to me.
Oh no! He's rolling to the ground
Catch him, now that he's found.
Where's bear now?
He's driving a car.
Wow, he can go really far.
Now he's back, I'm holding him tight.
I love him lots so I squeeze him
With all my might.

## Activities/Games/Props

### Flashlight Tag

Let the parents hold the flashlights and turn them on and off. The parents will sign *lights on* and *lights off* when they do the appropriate action. If they place the lights in different places on the floor or low on the wall, then the children can play tag with the light and try to catch it before it turns off again.

**Signs:** *lights on, lights off*

**Lights On**          **Lights Off**

### Peek-a-Boo

Use blankets or pillows and let the parents play peek-a-boo with their children. They may sign blanket, pillow, and/or hide.

**Signs:** *blanket, pillow, hide*

**Blanket**          **Pillow**          **Hide**

### Moon Match

Before class, make various patterned moons out of paper, two each of the same design. Hang one moon on a black piece of mural paper (which can be taped to the wall) and hand out the other moons to each child. (A star and moon template is provided in the appendix.) See if the children can find the match to their moon. You may substitute moons with any other nighttime object, such as teddy bears or stars.

### Bedtime Routine

Before class, print out pictures of things children do to get ready for bed: book, song, brush teeth, pajamas, bath, say I love you, wish on a star, lights off, etc. Help the children put them in order. You may tape them in order on the wall, put them in order on the floor, or put them in order from top to bottom in a pocket chart. Ask the children and their parents questions to determine their typical nighttime routine, for example, Do we put on our pajamas first and then take a bath? Do we turn off the light and then brush our teeth? Children/parents may answer back yes or no by saying and signing their answers.

**Signs:** *yes, no*

Yes          No

## Crafts

### Star Dots

**Materials Needed:** black construction paper, yellow dot paint

**Directions:** Let the children use the dot paints to make yellow stars in the night sky.

### Find the Stars and Moons

**Materials Needed:** Large dark blue or black mural paper, cut out moons from white paper and stars from yellow paper (star and moon template is provided in the appendix), clear or masking tape

**Directions:** Place cut out moons and stars around the room, and see if the children can find one. If they do, they may hang it in the sky with a piece of tape, helping to make a nighttime mural. It's better to roll the tape and place it behind the moon or star when placing it in the sky, so that the tape isn't visible in your mural when you're finished.

### Star Stickers

**Materials Needed:** coloring sheet of a nighttime scene, crayons, star stickers

**Directions:** Give each child a coloring sheet and some crayons. Let them color their coloring sheet. When they're done coloring, give them some star stickers to put up in their nighttime sky.

## Closing Songs

Italicized words should be signed.

### "The More We Sign Together"
### (Sing to the tune of "The More We Get Together.")

The *more* we *sign together, together, together,*
The *more* we *sign together,* the *happier* we'll be.
For *your friends* are *my friends* and *my friends* are *your friends,*
The *more* we *sign together* the *happier* we'll be.

**Signs:** *more, sign, together, happy, your, friends, my*

**More**

**Sign**

**Together**

**Happy**

**Your**

**Friends**

**My**

"Good-bye Friends"
(Sing to the tune of "Goodnight Ladies.")

*Good-bye friends, good-bye friends, good-bye friends,* we'll see you here *again.*

*Good-bye* [each child in the class gets a turn with his or her name here], we'll see you here *again.*

*Good-bye* everyone, *good-bye* everyone, *good-bye* everyone, we'll see you here *again.*

**Signs:** *good-bye, friends, see you, again*

**Good-bye**

**Friends**

**See You**

**Again**

Bedtime is a very important part of a baby's and toddler's day. Depending on how young they are, bedtime happens several times a day. Giving parents and young children the opportunity and knowledge to share bedtime signs along with their well-loved bedtime stories and songs is a wonderful gift to your patrons. The next chapter uses the theme mealtime, another very important part of babies' days.

# Glossary of Signs Used in Bedtime Theme

**Again**

**Baby**

**Bath**

**Bed**

**Blanket**

**Book**

**Break**

**Brush**

**Brush Teeth**

**Close Eyes**

**Day**

**Diamond**

# Glossary of Signs Used in Bedtime Theme

**Dreams**

**Eight**

**Fall**

**Five**

**Four**

**Friends**

**Glad/Happy**

**Good**

**Good-bye**

**Hello**

**Hide**

**Hug**

# Glossary of Signs Used in Bedtime Theme

**Hurt**

**I Love You**

**Kiss**

**Lights Off**

**Lights On**

**Love**

**Mom/Mother**

**Moon**

**More**

**My**

**Night**

**Nine**

# Glossary of Signs Used in Bedtime Theme

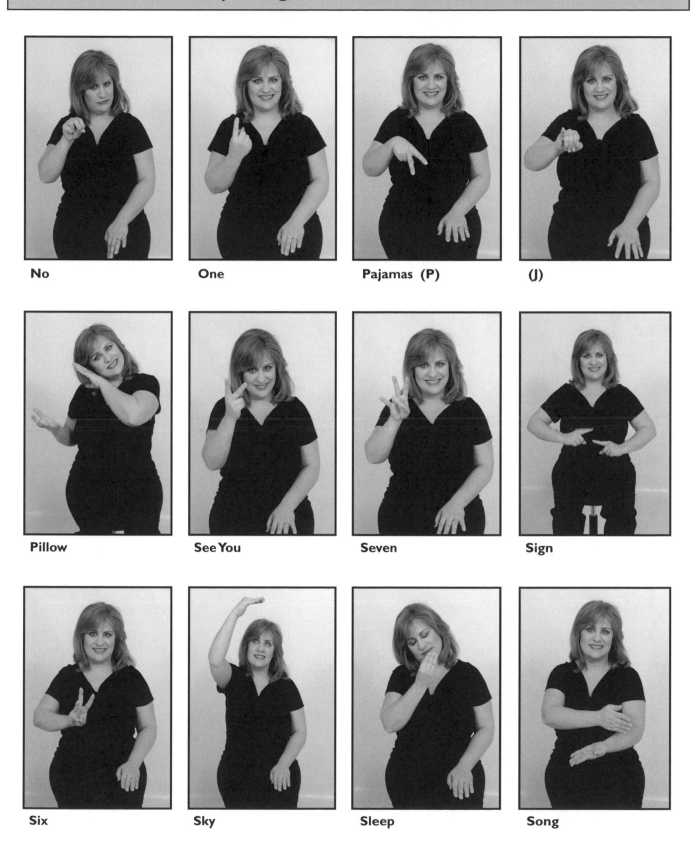

No

One

Pajamas (P)

(J)

Pillow

See You

Seven

Sign

Six

Sky

Sleep

Song

# Glossary of Signs Used in Bedtime Theme

**Star**

**Story**

**Ten**

**Three**

**Tired**

**Today**

**Together**

**Twinkle**

**Two**

**Up Above**

**Wash**

**Wind**

From *Once Upon a Sign: Using American Sign Language to Engage, Entertain, and Teach All Children* by Kim Taylor-DiLeva.
Santa Barbara, CA: Libraries Unlimited. Copyright © 2011.

# Glossary of Signs Used in Bedtime Theme

**Winter**

**Wonder**

**World**

**Yes**

**Your**

# Chapter 6

# Mealtime—Sample Rhyme and Sign for Babies/Toddlers

> **Signing Tip:** Babies' first signs are usually related to mealtime. Signs like *more, all done (finished)*, *milk*, and *eat* are often the first words signed by babies. Therefore, teaching mealtime signs is a great way for you to inform parents about signing. How helpful would it be for parents to know if their child wants more food or is all done, is still hungry or wants some water? Through signing, parents can find out the answers to these questions before the baby or toddler can actually tell them verbally.

As mentioned in the signing tip, babies' and toddlers' first signs are typically related to mealtime. This demonstrates how important mealtime is to young children; therefore, teaching a theme on mealtime is great to incorporate into your infant and toddler rhyme and sign storytime.

## Sample Lesson Plan for a 45-Minute Lesson

*Welcome Song—"Hello Friends"*

*Book—* Bear Wants More *by Karma Wilson*

*Song—"More Milk"*

*Activity—Who Stole the Cookie?*

*Book—The Water Hole by Graham Base*

*Puppets—Feed the Cookie Monster*

*Movement—"Pop! Pop! Pop!"*

*Closing Song—"The More We Sign Together"*

*Game—Parachute Popcorn*

*Activity—Pasta Playtime*

*Craft—Cookie Press*

*Closing Song—"Good-bye Friends"*

## Welcome Song

Signed words are shown in italics in the song and illustrated below.

### "Hello Friends" (Sing to the tune of "Goodnight Ladies.")

*Hello friends, hello friends, hello friends,* we're *glad* you're here *today.*
*Hello* [each child in the class gets a turn with his or her name here], we're *glad* you're here *today.*
*Hello* everyone, *hello* everyone, *hello* everyone, we're *glad* you're here *today.*

**Signs:** *hello, friends, glad, today*

| **Hello** | **Friends** | **Glad/Happy** | **Today** |

## Theme

Introduce the theme of the day—mealtime. You may want to introduce some commonly used signs right in the beginning, such as the following.

| **More** | **All Done/Finished** | **Eat/Food** |

## Stories

**Base, Graeme.** *The Water Hole.* **New York: Puffin, 2001.**
This book helps children count while introducing various types of animals. As the water hole that the animals share dries up, they must wait for rainfall to fill it again.

**Signs:** *water*

**Water**

**Carle, Eric.** *The Very Hungry Caterpillar.* **New York: Philomel Books, 1987.**
Caterpillar is very hungry and eats through a new food each day of the week. By the end of the week, he is a big fat caterpillar. What do you think he does next?

**Signs:** *hungry, apple, pears, plums, strawberries, oranges*

**Hungry**          **Apple**          **Pears**

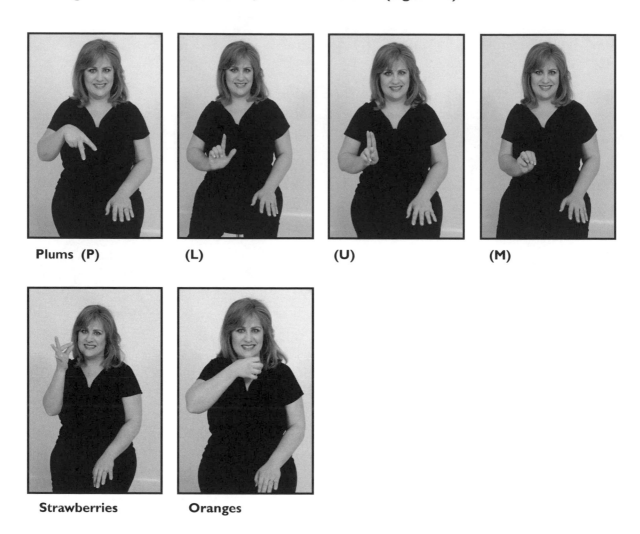

Plums (P)    (L)    (U)    (M)

Strawberries    Oranges

Carle, Eric. *Today Is Monday.* New York: Philomel Books, 1993.
Every day of the week a new food is eaten.

**Signs:** *beans, spaghetti, soup, meat, fish, chicken, ice cream*

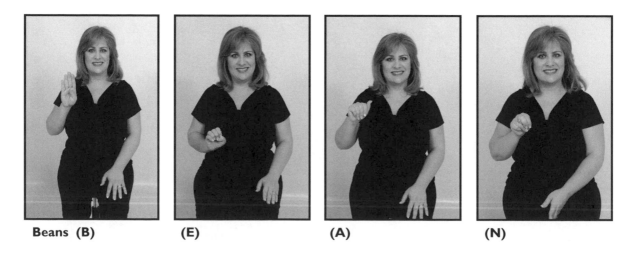

Beans (B)    (E)    (A)    (N)

**Spaghetti**

**Soup**

**Meat (Roast Beef)**

**Fish**

**Chicken (Sign Bird and then peck on your hand.)**

**Ice Cream**

**Doyle, Malachy.** *Hungry! Hungry! Hungry!* **Atlanta, GA: Peachtree Publishers, 2001.**

A goblin shows up in the front yard looking for something to eat. The boy is curious and asks lots of questions—to most of which the answer is hungry, hungry, hungry!

**Signs:** *hungry*

**Hungry**

Ericsson, Jennifer A. *No Milk*. New York: HarperTrophy, 1998.

Will this city boy figure out a way to get milk from the cow?

**Sign:** *milk*

**Milk**

Fleming, Denise. *Lunch*. New York: Henry Holt, 1992.

Mouse is hungry and eats lots of colorful vegetables and fruits.

**Signs:** *hungry, lunch (in the title), dinner*

**Hungry**                    **Lunch (sign Eat and Noon)**

**Dinner (sign Eat and Night)**

**Gelman, Rita Golden.** *More Spaghetti, I Say!* **New York: Scholastic, 1977.**

Freddy wants Minnie to play with him, but she is too busy having fun with her spaghetti.

**Signs:** *spaghetti, eat (eating), more*

**Spaghetti**                **Eat/Eating**                **More**

**Horacek, Petr.** *Strawberries Are Red.* **Somerville, MA: Candlewick Press , 2001.**
Each fruit, in a different color, makes a beautiful fruit salad.
**Signs:** *strawberries, oranges, bananas, apples, blueberries, grapes, fruit*
**Optional sign:** *salad.*

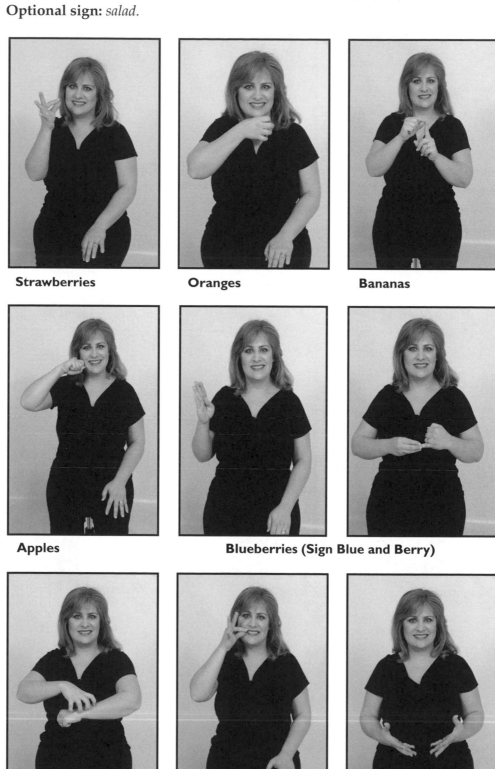

Strawberries     Oranges     Bananas

Apples     Blueberries (Sign Blue and Berry)

Grapes     Fruit     Salad

**Hutchins, Pat.** *Ten Red Apples*. **New York: Greenwillow Books, 1999.**

The farm animals each eat an apple off the tree. Will they save one for the farmer?

**Signs:** *apple*

**Optional sign:** *eat (for the word ate)*

**Apples**          **Eat/Ate**

**Munsch, Robert.** *More Pies!* **New York: Scholastic, 2002.**

Samuel wakes up really hungry. So hungry that he just can't get enough—until he enters a pie eating contest.

**Signs:** *hungry, more, eat, tummy hurts*

**Hungry**          **More**          **Eat**          **Tummy Hurts**

**Snow, Pegeen.** *Eat Your Peas, Louise!* **Danbury, CT: Children's Press, 1985.**

Louise's mom tries many different ways to get Louise to eat her peas.

**Signs:** *eat*

**Optional sign:** *please.*

**Eat**                    **Please**

**Willems, Mo.** *The Pigeon Finds a Hot Dog.* **New York: Hyperion Books, 2004.**

Pigeon finds a hot dog and is ready to eat it, until duckling shows up asking questions.

**Signs:** *hot dog*

**Hot Dog**

**Wilson, Karma.** *Bear Wants More.* **New York: Margaret K. McElderry Books, 2003.**

Even though his forest friends help Bear find more food, Bear still wants more!

**Signs:** *more*

**Optional sign:** *eat*

**More**          **Eat**

**Yolen, Jane, and Mark Teague.** *How Do Dinosaurs Eat Their Food?* **New York: Blue Sky Press, 2005.**

Does dinosaur eat using his manners, or does he eat like a messy dinosaur?

**Signs:** *eat*

**Optional signs:** *please, thank you, more*

**Eat**       **Please**       **Thank You**       **More**

## Songs

Italicized words should be signed.

**de Azevedo Coleman, Rachel. "Eat and Drink." In** *Baby Signing Time! Vol. 1: It's Baby Signing Time Music CD.* **Two Little Hands Productions, 2007.**

**Signs:** *eat, all done, drink, crackers, water, cereal, milk, bananas, juice*

**Eat**

**All Done (Finished)**

**Drink**

**Crackers**

**Water**

**Cereal**

**Milk**                    **Bananas**                    **Juice**

"More Milk." In *Li'L Pick Me Up! Fun Songs for Learning ASL Signs.* CD. Sign2Me/ Northlight Communications, 2009.

**Signs:** *milk, all gone, juice, crackers, water, apples, cheese*

**Milk**              **All Gone**              **Juice**              **Crackers**

**Water**                    **Apples**                    **Cheese**

"Sometimes When I Am Hungry." In *Li'L Pick Me Up! Fun Songs for Learning ASL Signs.* CD. Sign2Me/Northlight Communications, 2009.

**Signs:** *hungry, cracker, please, thirsty, water, apple, milk, banana, thank you*

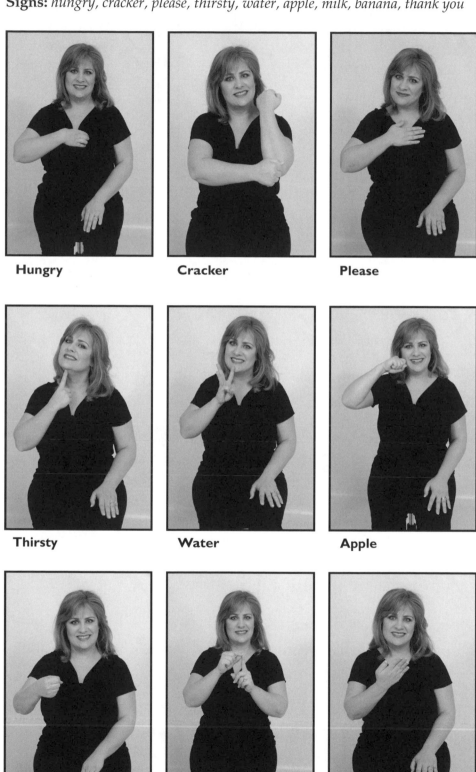

| | | |
|---|---|---|
| **Hungry** | **Cracker** | **Please** |
| **Thirsty** | **Water** | **Apple** |
| **Milk** | **Banana** | **Thank You** |

The Wiggles. "Fruit Salad." In *Hot Potatoes: Best of the Wiggles Music CD*. Koch Records, 2009.

**Signs:** *fruit, salad, bananas, grapes, apples, melons, eat*

**Fruit**

**Salad**

**Banana**

**Grapes**

**Apple**

**Melon**

**Eat**

de Azevedo Coleman, Rachel. "That Tastes Good." In *Baby Signing Time! Vol. 4 : Let's Be Friends Music CD.* Two Little Hands Productions, 2009.

**Signs:** *apple, pear, fruit, vegetable, carrot, peach*

**Apple**

**Pear**

**Fruit**

**Vegetable**

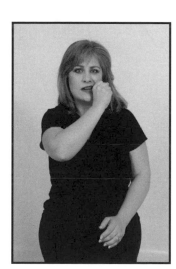

**Carrot**

**Peach**

## "This Is the Way We Eat Our Apples"
### (Sung to the tune of "Here We Go Round the Mulberry Bush.")

This is the way we *eat* our *apples*, *eat* our *apples*, *eat* our *apples*,
This is the way we *eat* our *apples*, early in the morning.

Continue with other verses and foods, for example, bananas, grapes, oranges. For other foods that you choose to use, see the glossary at the end of this chapter.

**Signs:** *eat, apple*

**Eat**

**Apple**

## "I Like Fruit" (Sing to the tune of "Twinkle, Twinkle Little Star.")

I like *fruit*, yes it's true.

I like it in a *salad*, how about you?

I like *apples* and *oranges*, too.

I like *bananas* and *pears*, too.

I like *fruit*, yes it's true.

I like it in a *salad*, how about you?

**Signs:** *fruit, salad, apples, oranges, bananas, pears*

**Fruit**

**Salad**

**Apples**

**Oranges**

**Bananas**

**Pears**

## "F-R-U-I-T" (Sing to the tune of "B-I-N-G-O.")

There is a *food* I love to *eat*.

It's yummy and healthy, too.

F-R-U-I-T, F-R-U-I-T, F-R-U-I-T,

Is just the *food* for me.

Continue a second time with a clap in place of the F, a third time with claps for the F and R, until you are clapping every letter in the word fruit.

**Signs:** *food/eat*

**Food/Eat**

"Table Manners" (Sing to the tune of "I'm a Little Teapot.")

I use my table manners, yes I do,
*More*, *please*, and *thank you*, too.
Manners are important, I know it's true.
Saying polite words at dinner time to you.

I use my manners, yes I do,
*More*, *please*, and *thank you*, too.

**Signs:** *more, please, thank you*

**More**              **Please**              **Thank You**

# Movement

### "This Is the Way We Bake the Cake"
### (Sing to the tune of "Here We Go Round the Mulberry Bush.")

This is the way we bake the *cake*, bake the *cake*, bake the *cake*,
This is the way we bake the *cake*, so we can *eat* it up!
This is the way we make the *bread*, make the *bread*, make the *bread*,
This is the way we make the *bread*, so we can *eat* it up!
This is the way we toss the *salad*, toss the *salad*, toss the *salad*,
This is the way we toss the *salad*, so we can *eat* it up!
This is the way we roll out the *pizza*, roll out the *pizza*, roll out the *pizza*,
This is the way we roll out the *pizza*, so we can *eat* it up!
This is the way we press the *cookies*, press the *cookies*, press the *cookies*,

This is the way we press the *cookies*, so we can *eat* it up!

This is the way we stir the *spaghetti*, stir the *spaghetti*, stir the *spaghetti*,

This is the way we stir the *spaghetti*, so we can *eat* it up!

Add the motions in addition to the food signs to make this song even more fun. Also feel free to add any other motions and foods that you can think of to keep this song going longer. Parents may hold babies' hands and help them make the motions.

**Signs:** *cake, eat, bread, salad, pizza, cookies, spaghetti*

**Cake**

**Eat**

**Bread**

**Salad**

**Pizza**

**Cookies**

**Spaghetti**

### "Pop, Pop, Pop!"

Light the fire for the pot, *Pop, Pop, Pop!*

Pour the corn into the pot, *Pop, Pop, Pop!*

Shake and shake and shake, *Pop, Pop, Pop!*

Now it's too hot, *Pop, Pop, Pop!*

So what have you got? *Pop, Pop, POPCORN!*

Children may jump for the word "Pop" and then act out the other actions. Everyone signs *popcorn* at the end.

**Signs:** *popcorn*

**Popcorn**

### "Apples in the Basket"

There are *apples* in the basket, so I see,

Five for you and five for me.

Let's jump each time we put one in:

1 (jump), 1 (jump), 2 (jump), 2 (jump), 3 (jump), 3 (jump), 4 (jump), 4 (jump), 5 (jump), 5 (jump)

You can keep doing this activity by replacing "jump" with any other action word you'd like to use.

**Signs:** *apple*

**Apple**

## Puppets

### Feed the Monster Cookies

**Materials Needed:** Monster puppet and pretend cookies (plastic, or you can make them of cardboard), orany puppet and any pretend food available

**Directions:** Your puppet is really hungry. Have your puppet tell the children that he or she is really hungry and ask for food. Let the children feed the food to your puppet (one at a time). You may want to cut open a hole where the puppet's mouth is so that the food actually goes into its mouth. If you don't have much of one type of food, hand out various foods to the children and your puppet can say that he or she feels like eating an apple and ask, Does anyone have an apple that I can eat? Of course when the puppet is eating the children love the puppet to make eating sounds.

## Activities/Games/Props

### Let's Make a Fruit Salad

Use plastic fruit to make a fruit salad. Sign the different types of fruit you add to your fruit salad (see the glossary at the end of this chapter for the signs). Children may add a piece of plastic fruit and then get a turn to stir the fruit salad. To add even more fun, sing and/or play the music for the song "Fruit Salad" by the Wiggles (cited in the song section of this chapter).

"Who Stole the Cookie?"

Who stole the *cookie* from the cookie jar?

Who, me? Yes, you!

Couldn't be! Then who?


Class: (child's name) stole the *cookie* from the cookie jar.

Child: Who, me?

Class: Yes, you!

Child: Couldn't be! Then who?

The child chooses the next person to have stolen the cookie. For little ones, parents may say the child's part and choose the next child. Continue for as many children as there are in your storytime.

**Signs:** *cookie*

**Cookie**

### "Patty Cake"

Patty cake, patty cake, baker's man,

Bake me a cake as fast as you can.

Roll it, pat it, mark it with a B,

And put it in the oven for Baby and me.

You can do this over several times by substituting B/Baby for each child in the class. For example:

Patty cake, patty cake, baker's man,

Bake me a *cake* as fast as you can.

Roll it, pat it, mark it with a J,

And put it in the oven for John and me.

**Signs:** *cake*

**Cake**

### Pasta Playtime

Put different kinds of pasta (uncooked) in a big clear tub or basket. Let the children play with a few toys (preferably plastic food) in the pasta. They may hide their orange (for example) and then try to find it. Babies love to feel the pasta on their hands—it's kind of like getting to play in the water or a sandbox.

### Parachute Popcorn

Put plastic or soft balls on top of a children's toy parachute that is laid out on the ground. Have the parents make the parachute go up and down while they sit on the ground and watch the balls pop up and down like popcorn.

### Kitchen Playtime

Have an assortment of kitchen items available for the children to play with and give them five minutes or so to just free play with the various items. If you have a plastic kitchen set for kids, that would be best (plastic pans, pots, etc.), but plastic storage containers, spoons, etc., from your own kitchen may be used.

For more food-related activities, you may want to look at *Story Times Good Enough to Eat!* by Melissa Rossetti Folini. It has some other great suggestions for books to read and explains how to make edible items that look like objects that go along with the story.

## Crafts

### Cookie Press

**Materials Needed:** cookie cutters, construction paper—at least one for each child, washable and nontoxic paint

**Directions:** Let the children press the cookie cutters in the paint and then onto their paper to see what beautiful creations they can make.

### Finger Paint Pizza

**Materials Needed:** construction paper, one or two cans of pizza sauce, bowls to put the sauce into, paper towels or wipes for cleanup

**Directions:** Pour the pizza sauce into the bowls so that the children can easily reach it. Let the children dip their fingers into the pizza sauce and then draw a picture with their fingers on their piece of paper. Make sure you have paper towels or wipes available for cleaning messy hands! You may want to have parents double check the ingredients on the can to make sure there are no allergy issues.

## Closing Songs

Italicized words should be signed.

### "The More We Sign Together" (Sing to the tune of "The More We Get Together.")

The *more* we *sign together*, *together*, *together*,
The *more* we *sign together*, the *happier* we'll be.
For *your friends* are *my friends* and *my friends* are *your friends*,
The *more* we *sign together*, the *happier* we'll be.

**Signs:** *more, sign, together, happy, your, friends, my*

**More**    **Sign**    **Together**    **Happy**

**Your**

**Friends**

**My**

## "Good-bye Friends" (Sing to the tune of "Goodnight Ladies.")

*Good-bye friends, good-bye friends, good-bye friends*, we'll *see you* here *again*.
*Good-bye* [each child in the class gets a turn with his or her name here], we'll *see you* here *again*.
*Good-bye* everyone, *good-bye* everyone, *good-bye* everyone, we'll *see you* here *again*.

**Signs:** *good-bye, friends, see you, again*

**Good-bye**

**Friends**

**See You**

**Again**

Because babies eat and sleep most of the day and take a bath usually at least once a day, we've covered a good portion of your young patrons' day just through these three rhyme and signs. After you've done these three, you may want to take a theme you are already using and start looking at your books and songs for some that can easily incorporate sign language. Now that you're comfortable adding sign language into your baby and toddler storytimes, the next chapter looks at sign language programs for preschool and primary children.

# Glossary of Signs Used in Mealtime Theme

**Again**

**All Done/Finished**

**All Gone**

**Apple**

**Beans (B)**

**(E)**

**(A)**

**(N)**

**Bananas**

**(Sign Blue and Berries)**

**Bread**

# Glossary of Signs Used in Mealtime Theme

**Cake**          **Carrot**          **Cereal**          **Cheese**

**Chicken**          **Cookies**          **Corn**

**Crackers**          **Dinner (Sign Eat and Night)**          **Drink**

# Glossary of Signs Used in Mealtime Theme

**Eat**

**Fish**

**Friends**

**Fruit**

**Glad/Happy**

**Good-bye**

**Grapes**

**Hello**

**Hungry**

**Ice Cream**

**Juice**

**Lunch (Sign Eat as Shown Above and Noon)**

# Glossary of Signs Used in Mealtime Theme

**Meat**

**Milk**

**Melon**

**More**

**My**

**Orange**

**Peach**

**Pear**

**Peas**

**Pizza**

**Please**

**Popcorn**

# Glossary of Signs Used in Mealtime Theme

 Plum (P)

 (L)

 (U)

 (M)

 Salad

 See You

 Sign

 Soup

 Spaghetti

 Strawberries

 Thank You

 Thirsty

# Glossary of Signs Used in Mealtime Theme

**Today**

**Together**

**Tummy Hurts**

**Vegetable**

**Water**

**Watermelon**

**Your**

# Part III

## Programs for Preschool and Primary Children (Ages 3–7)

# Chapter 7

# Working with Preschool and Primary Children

You're probably already doing some fantastic storytimes for preschoolers, and this book gives you another teaching tool to help make your storytimes more engaging and entertaining for the children and their parents who attend.

The next few chapters provide some examples of popular storytime themes and suggested books, songs, stories, activities, movement, puppets, and more that you can do while integrating sign language. You will also see what words to sign, as well as the signs to go along with them.

At some point you will want to start integrating sign language into the storytime themes that you are already doing. Following are some steps to keep in mind, which will make adding sign language to any theme you choose much easier.

## 1. Don't Try to Sign Everything!

Make it easy on yourself by just signing the keywords, the most important words or the words that repeat in the story. In the animal and color examples in the upcoming chapters, there are signs for every color and every animal. However, in the friendship theme, only the most important (and/or repeating) words in the book or in each line of the songs are signed. Children will be able to pick up on sign language much more easily if they sign just a few keywords, not everything. In addition, it will be easier for you to learn and teach when you are just signing a few keywords and not everything. Make it easy and just pick out a few keywords to sign. I typically recommend starting with just one or two. Once you are comfortable, add some more.

## 2. Don't Overwhelm Yourself!

There are many activities in this chapter, many more than you can possibly do in a 45-minute storytime. I did this so that you can pick and choose the songs you are most comfortable with, the activities you have the materials for, and the books you have at your library, but most important, so that you can choose the books, songs, and activities that have the number of signs you are comfortable with. To start, choose the books with only one or two signs that go along with them, choose the songs that have only a few signs, etc. It is easy to look at the various signs and become overwhelmed. You don't have to learn them all. Just learn the few that you need for the books and songs that you want to do.

Remember that you don't have to learn all of and become fluent in ASL to start using it in your storytime. Start with a few signs, at a pace that you are comfortable with, and then the next time you do that theme, add a few new signs/stories/songs. Pretty soon you'll be impressed with how many signs you know and can integrate into your storytimes.

## 3. Use Your Resources!

Don't forget to use the resources that appear in the back of this book. I highly recommend using the online dictionaries, which have videos of people making the signs. The videos makes it easy for you to figure out which way your hand should move, or which finger to use to make a particular sign. These resources can help you make sure you are teaching each ASL sign correctly. You can also look up signs that don't appear in this book that you want to use in your other storytimes. Choose your theme, choose the book you want to use, then pick the keywords or repeating words and look them up in an ASL online dictionary. Learn the signs, and you're ready to go!

## 4. Don't Teach American Sign Language as a Separate Thing!

Don't feel that you have to teach ASL signs at the beginning of each storytime and then conduct your program as you usually do. The key to engaging and entertaining the children, and getting all the great benefits from using sign language with hearing children, is to INTEGRATE it into your already established program. Teaching sign language as a separate program or lesson and not integrating it won't give you great results. Follow the directions and examples provided and integrate sign language into your already established programs.

## 5. Use Facial Expressions!

Last but not least, facial expressions are very important in sign language. Because deaf and many hard of hearing people cannot hear the inflections in voices (loud or soft, harsh or gentle), they rely on people's faces to tell them what is meant. For example, if I say, "no, no, no" in a playful way to a toddler one time, but yell "no" as the child reaches for an electrical outlet, the meaning of the word *no* and the intensity with which I mean it change. It is important when using sign language signs to show the meaning of the word with your face where necessary. Just as in a read-aloud, when there are quotations we read as if we are actually the person talking, to help children understand the meaning. When using an ASL sign, the face helps to convey the meaning, so remember to show in your face how the characters feel or how they are saying the words, along with your signs.

## 6. Stay as True to the Language as You Can!

Remember that we are using signs from another language. In essence we are borrowing from an already established language and culture and using it in our programs. To remain respectful of that language, it is important to stay as true to it as you can. If using a sign, don't make up a gesture, but actually use the resources available to you in print and online to look up the actual sign, so that you will be as accurate as possible.

Just as many languages have variations in words used (soda vs. pop) or accents in various parts of a country, ASL also has variations. Although the resources are wonderful, people in your location may make that sign a little bit differently. That's okay. Just use the one you have learned, from the resources you have, and if someone in your area shows you another way—that's okay, too!

These tips will help you take your already established storytimes and integrate ASL signs easily, comfortably, and accurately. Just remember to start slowly and at the level that you are comfortable with. The parents and children will be thrilled even if you only teach them one or two signs at first, so start easily and comfortably.

# Chapter 8

# Friendship Storytime with Sign Language

---

**Signing Tip:** Children can sign to each other to solve their conflicts. Early childhood educators who sign with the children in their care report fewer instances of biting and hitting as a result of the children being able to sign with each other. Signs like *my turn*, *your turn*, and *share* are particularly helpful.

---

   Friendship is a great theme to use in the library, especially as you are coming back into your fall programs and have some new faces at your storytime. It can promote making friends, having friends, sharing, caring, playing nicely, etc. It is often one of the first taught in early childhood programs in August/September when a new class is forming and the children are meeting each other for the first time.

   Your current storytime is most likely incorporating books, songs, movement, and maybe even some puppets, activities, and/or crafts. This chapter takes each of these elements and shows how you can easily incorporate sign language in every part of your storytime. There are many suggested books, games, songs, movement activities, and crafts using the friendship theme, along with the signs to use with them.

## Sample Lesson Plan for a 45-Minute Lesson

Again, if you wish, replace these books, songs, and activities with those you are comfortable with.

*Welcome Song—"Hello Friends"*

*Book—May I Bring a Friend? by Beatrice Schenk DeRegniers*

*Song—"Friend of Mine?"*

*Gross Motor Movement—If You're Friendly and You Know It*

*Book—My Best Friend by Pat Hutchins*

*Puppets—Five Little Friends*

*Book—Time to Say "Please" by Mo Willems*

*Closing Song—"The More We Sign Together"*

*Game—Musical Shares*

*Craft—Friendship Bracelet*

*Closing Song—"Good-bye Friends"*

## Welcome Song

Signed words are shown in italics in the song and illustrated below.

"Hello Friends" (Sing to the tune of "Goodnight Ladies.")

*Hello friends, hello friends, hello friends,* we're *glad* you're here *today.*

*Hello* (each child in the class gets a turn with their name in here), we're *glad* you're here *today.*

Hello everyone, *hello* everyone, *hello* everyone, we're *glad* you're here *today.*

**Signs:** *hello, friends, glad, today*

**Hello**

**Friends**

**Glad/Happy**

**Today**

# Theme

Introduce the theme of the day—friendship. During this time you may discuss what the word "friendship" means and what it means to be a good friend.

# Stories

**DeRegniers, Beatrice Schenk.** *May I Bring a Friend?* **New York: Aladdin, 1974.**
In this story, the King and Queen invite a little boy to visit them, and he asks to bring a friend each time. It is always a different kind of animal, which the King and Queen welcome.

**Signs:** *friend*

**Optional signs:** *days of the week*

| **Friend** | **Sunday** | **Monday** | **Tuesday** |

| **Wednesday** | **Thursday** | **Friday** | **Saturday** |

**Heine, Helme.** *Friends.* **New York: Aladdin, 1997.**

Three farm animals learn that although they have to be apart sometimes, they will always be together again because they are best friends.

**Signs:** *friends*

**Friends**

**Hutchins, Pat.** *My Best Friend.* **1st ed. New York: Greenwillow Books, 1993.**

This story teaches that although two friends may have different qualities, both are equally important to their friendship, teaching children that their special skills are just as important as another's.

**Signs:** *friends*

**Friends**

**Keller, Holly.** *Help! A Story of Friendship.* **New York: HarperCollins, 2007.**

This story describes how various animals have certain skills that can be used to help other animals when they are in trouble, showing children how they can help each other.

**Signs:** *friends, help*

**Friends**

**Help**

**Lionni, Leo.** *It's Mine!* **New York: Dragonfly Books, 1996.**

Three frogs constantly argue over who owns certain things, such as the water, but when they are faced with obstacles, they realize that it is most important to not be selfish and to work together.

**Signs:** *mine, ours*

**Mine**

**Ours**

**Lipmiacka, Ewa.** *It's Mine.* **London: Little Tigers Press, 2004.**

Two brothers do not want to share any of their belongings.

**Signs:** *share*

**Share**

**Llewellyn, Claire.** *Why Should I Share?* **Hauppage, NY: Barron's Educational Series, 2005.**

In this story, Tim does not like to share with his sister, but when he sees how fun sharing can be, he changes his mind.

**Signs:** *share*

**Share**

**Mayer, Cassie.** *Making Friends.* **Portsmouth, NH: Heinemann Educational Books, 2007.**

This book intends to help children through teaching them important principles such as sharing and obeying rules.

**Signs:** *friend*

**Friend**

**Scott, Elaine.** *Friends!* **New York: Atheneum, 2000.**

*Friends!* explores all aspects of friendship by presenting children with various scenarios on how to solve problems, such as including others and resolving disagreements.

**Signs:** *friends*

**Friends**

**Senning, Cindy Post, and Peggy Post.** *Emily's Sharing and Caring Book.* **New York: Collins, 2008.**

The title says it all—the book teaches children the importance of sharing and other manners.

**Signs:** *share*

**Share**

**Waters, Jennifer.** *Be a Good Friend.* **Mankato, MN: Spyglass Books, 2002.**

In this book, Waters depicts the qualities that make a good friend.

**Signs:** *friend*

**Friend**

**Willems, Mo.** *Time to Say "Please"!* **New York: Hyperion Book CH, 2005.**

> Using humor, Willems teaches children the importance of using good manners to get what they want.

**Signs:** *please, thank you*

**Optional sign:** *sorry*

**Please**

**Thank You**

**Sorry**

## Songs

Italicized words should be signed.

**"Friend of Mine."** In *Preschool Education.com: Discover the Fun in Learning.* **Preschool Education, 1997–2010. Available at www.preschooleducation.com/sfriend.shtml. Accessed April 29, 2010.**

> Sung to the tune of "Mary Had a Little Lamb," participants introduce the person sitting next to them and say that child's name. You may keep going around the room until everyone has been introduced. This is a great way for the children to learn each other's names in the class, in addition to learning the signs for *friend* and *meet*.

**Signs:** *meet, friend*

**Meet**

**Friend**

de Azevedo Coleman, Rachel. "Magic Words." In *Signing Time! Songs Vol. 1-3 Music CD.* Two Little Hands Productions, 2002.

**Signs:** *I, magic, friends, nice, please, share, your turn, my turn, thank you*

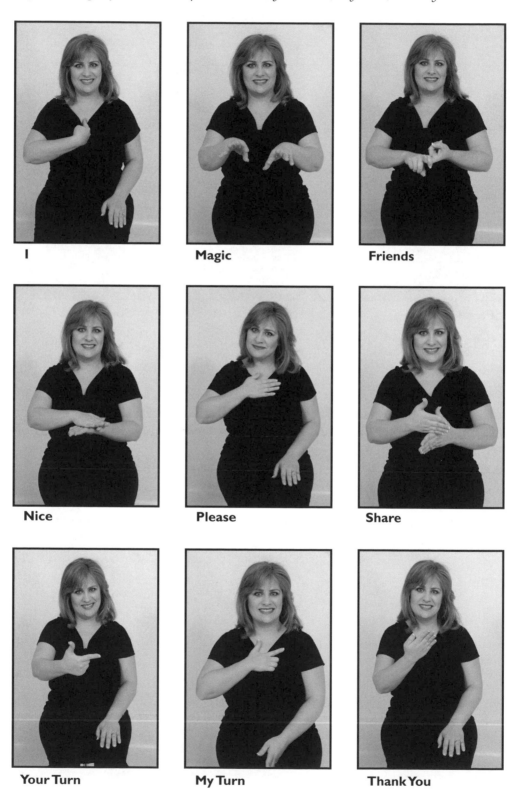

I     Magic     Friends

Nice     Please     Share

Your Turn     My Turn     Thank You

"We Are Friends" (Sing to the tune of "Three Blind Mice.")

We are *friends*, we are *friends*,
See how we *share*, see how we *share*,
Every day we play so *nice*, sharing all the things we *like*.
First it's *your turn* and then it's *mine (sign my turn)*,
We are *friends*, we are *friends*.

**Signs:** *friends, share, nice, like, your turn, my turn*

**Friends**

**Share**

**Nice**

**Like**

**Your Turn**

**My Turn**

## "Storytime Friends" (Sing to the tune of "Frere Jacques.")

*Where* is _____? [child's name is said in the blank]

*Where* is _____? [child's name is said in the blank]

*There* he(she) is.

*There* he(she) is.

You are in our *storytime* [sign *story*],

You are in our *storytime*,

We are *friends.* We are *friends.*

**Signs:** *where, there, story, friends*

| **Where** | **There** | **Story** | **Friends** |

## "Hello to You" (Sing to the tune of "B-I-N-G-O.")

There is a *library* that has a *boy/girl* and his/her *name* is [child's name].

*Hello* to you, *hello* to you, *hello* to you.

*Stand* up and spin around.

**Signs:** *library, boy, girl, name, hello, stand*

| **Library** | **Boy** | **Girl** | **Name** |

**Hello**

**Stand**

## "That's What Friends Do" (Sing to the tune of "Row, Row, Row Your Boat.")

*Share, share, share* our things.
It's easy, it's *true.*
*Your turn, my turn,*
*Your turn, my turn,*
That's what *friends* do.

**Signs:** *share, true, your turn, my turn, friends*

**Share**

**True**

**Your Turn**

**My Turn**          **Friends**

## Movement

Italicized words should be signed.

### "If You're Friends and You Know It"
### (Sing to the tune of "If You're Happy and You Know It.")

If you're *friends* and you know it,
clap your hands (clap, clap).
If you're *friends* and you know it,
clap your hands (clap, clap).

If you're *friends* and you know it,
and you really *want* to show it,
If you're *friends* and you know it,
clap your hands (clap, clap)!

If you *share* and you know it,
take a bow,
If you *share* and you know it,
take a bow.

If you *share* and you know it,
and you really want to show it,
If you *share* and you know it,
take a bow!

If you *take turns* and you know it,
turn around.
If you *take turns* and you know it,
turn around.

If you *take turns* and you know it,
and you really want to show it,
If you *take turns* and you know it,
turn around.

If you say *please* and you know it,
touch your toes.
If you say *please* and you know it,
touch your toes.

If you say *please* and you know it,
and you really want to show it,
If you say *please* and you know it,
touch your toes.

If you say *thank you* and you know it,
walk on tippy toes.
If you say *thank you* and you know it,
walk on tippy toes.

If you say *thank you* and you know it,
and you really want to show it,
If you say *thank you* and you know it,
walk on tippy toes.

If you say *excuse me* and you know it,
touch the sky,
If you say *excuse me* and you know it,
touch the sky.

If you say *excuse me* and you know it,
and you really want to show it,
if you say *excuse me* and you know it,
touch the sky.

If you're *friendly* and you know it,
shake a friend's hand.
If you're *friendly* and you know it,
shake a friend's hand.

If you're *friendly* and you know it,
and you really want to show it,
If you're *friendly* and you know it,
shake a friend's hand!

**Signs:** *friendly, share, take turns, please, thank you, excuse me, friends*

**Friendly**

**Share**

**Take Turns**

**Please**

**Thank You**

**Excuse Me**

**Friends**

**"Let's Find a Friend."** In *Preschool Education.com: Discover the Fun in Learning*. Preschool Education, 1997–2010. Available at www.preschooleducation.com/sfriend.shtml. Accessed April 29, 2010.

Sung to tune of "The Farmer in the Dell," this movement activity gives children the chance to interact with each other. All the children stand in a big circle, with one student standing in the middle. The child in the middle proceeds to pick a friend from the outside circle to join him or her in the middle, while everyone sings the words to the song. Great fun.

**Signs:** *friend*

**Friend**

**"Friend of Mine."** In *Preschool Education.com: Discover the Fun in Learning*. Preschool Education, 1997–2010. Available at www.preschooleducation.com/sfriend.shtml. Accessed April 29, 2010.

This is a great song to jump, sway, stomp, and add any other fun kind of movement to. I highly recommend using this song, because it gives children the opportunity to sign the word "friend" as they participate in as many different kinds of movement as you can come up with.

**Signs:** *friend*

**Friend**

## Puppets

Italicized words should be signed. Use five finger puppets on one hand and sign with the other.

### "Five Little Friends" (Sing to the tune of "Five Little Ducks.")

Five little *friends* went out to *play*,
Over the hills on a *sunny* day,
One little *friend* said, "I can't *stay*,"
And only four *friends* stayed to *play*.

Four little *friends* went out to *play*,
Over the hills on a *sunny* day,
One little *friend* said, "I can't *stay*,"
And only three *friends* stayed to *play*.

Three little *friends* went out to *play*,
Over the hills on a *sunny* day,
One little *friend* said, "I can't *stay*,"
And only two *friends* stayed to *play*.

Two little *friends* went out to *play*,
Over the hills on a *sunny* day,
One little *friend* said, "I can't *stay*,"
And only one *friend* stayed to *play*.

One little *friend* went out to *play*,
Over the hills on a *sunny* day,
One little *friend* said, "I can't *stay*,"
And then there were no *friends* out to *play*.

**Signs:** *friend, play, sunny, stay*

**Friend**          **Play**          **Sunny**          **Stay**

## Activities/Games/Props

"Musical Shares." In *Preschool Education.com: Discover the Fun in Learning.* Preschool
    Education, 1997–2010. Available at www.preschooleducation.com/gfriend.shtml.
    Accessed April 29, 2010.

> Similar to musical chairs, but with a chair taken out each time the music stops instead
> of a child. Children are learning how to share a chair with each other. Before starting
> the music again, everyone signs "share your chair" together.

**Signs:** *share, your, chair*

**Share**          **Your**          **Chair**

### Beanbag Toss

> Make sign language flashcards by copying and enlarging some of the friendship signs
> shown in the glossary at the end of this chapter. Lay out the flashcards on the floor.
> Each participant gets a turn to throw the beanbag onto a flashcard. Have the rest of the
> participants close their eyes and not watch. Once the person lands his or her beanbag
> on a card, he or she signs the word for the rest of the children and the children have to
> guess which one they landed on.

**Signs:** *the ones on your assorted flashcards*

### Mirror, Mirror

> Pair up your participants and have them mirror each other's signs. Participants take
> turns being the signer and the mirror. Explain that the mirror is also a talking mirror
> like the one in "Sleeping Beauty." They have to tell the person the sign they are making.

## Crafts

"Friendship Bracelet." In *Preschool Education.com: Discover the Fun in Learning*. Preschool Education, 1997–2010. Available at www.preschooleducation.com/ afriend.shtml. Accessed April 29, 2010.

Participants may make friendship bracelets out of colored round cereal. They may give them to friends in their class or take home to share with another friend (if they don't eat them first).

"Friendship Mural." In *Preschool Education.com: Discover the Fun in Learning*. Preschool Education, 1997–2010. Available at www.preschooleducation.com/afriend.shtml. Accessed April 29, 2010.

Use the children's handprints to make a large flower. Title it "Friendships bloom in our library" and hang it in your children's department for everyone to see.

## Closing Songs

Italicized words should be signed.

### "The More We Sign Together"\
### (Sing to the tune of "The More We Get Together.")

The *more* we *sign together*, *together*, *together*,

The *more* we *sign together*, the *happier* we'll be.

For *your friends* are *my friends* and *my friends* are *your friends*,

The *more* we *sign together* the *happier* we'll be.

**Signs:** *more, sign, together, happy, your, friends, my*

| **More** | **Sign** | **Together** | **Happy** |

**Your**

**Friends**

**My**

"Good-bye Friends" (Sing to the tune of "Goodnight Ladies.")

*Good-bye friends, good-bye friends, good-bye friends,* we'll *see you* here *again.*

*Good-bye* [each child in the class gets a turn with his or her name here], we'll *see you* here *again.*

*Good-bye* everyone, *good-bye* everyone, *good-bye* everyone, we'll *see you* here *again.*

**Signs:** *good-bye, friends, see you, again*

**Good-bye**

**Friends**

**See You**

**Again**

Learning how to make friends, build friendships, and be social is very important to preschoolers, primary school-age children, their parents, and their teachers. A nice added benefit to teaching sign language in a friendship storytime theme is that the children may make new friends in the storytime and then have a secret, silent language they can share with each other. The next chapter looks at the theme colors, another topic that parents and teachers want primary and preschool children to know. Including sign language in a theme on colors will help children learn their colors, and you'll be helping the parents teach their young children.

# Glossary of Signs Used in Friendship Theme

**Again**

**Boy**

**Chair**

**Friday**

**Excuse Me**

**Friends**

**Friendly**

**Girl**

**Glad/Happy**

**Good-bye**

**Hello**

# Glossary of Signs Used in Friendship Theme

**Help**      **I**      **Library**      **Like**

**Magic**      **Meet**      **Mine**      **Monday**

**More**      **My**      **My Turn**      **Name**

# Glossary of Signs Used in Friendship Theme

**Nice**

**Ours**

**Play**

**Please**

**Saturday**

**See You**

**Side**

**Sign**

**Share**

**Sorry**

**Stand**

**Stay**

# Glossary of Signs Used in Friendship Theme

**Story**

**Sunday**

**Sunny**

**Take Turns**

**Thank You**

**There**

**This**

**Thursday**

**Today**

**Together**

**True**

**Tuesday**

# Glossary of Signs Used in Friendship Theme

**Wednesday**

**Where**

**Your**

**Your Turn**

# Chapter 9

# Colors Storytime with Sign Language

> **Signing Tip:** Not all children learn by being told about something. In fact, the cone of experience theory of Edgar Dale states that we remember on average only 10 percent of what we hear but 90 percent of what we say and do. When children sign with you they get to hear new words, see new words, say new words, and create new words, therefore helping them learn and remember new things much more easily.

Using sign language when working with colors can be particularly useful with preschoolers and for the adults helping to teach them. Sign language can help teach the many different colors and even reinforce the colors that some children may already know. Color is a common theme used by early childhood educators, and when you do a theme on colors in the library and use the signs to go along with them, you help children learn colors and be better able to use them and recognize them when they are outside the library.

This chapter shows how songs, games, and other activities about colors may easily be incorporated into your library storytime. You will find many suggested books, songs, games, and crafts that focus on colors.

## Sample Lesson Plan for a 45-Minute Lesson

Again, if you wish, substitute books, songs, and activities with which you are comfortable for those listed here.

*Welcome Song—"Hello Friends"*

*Book—City Colors by Zoran Milich*

*Song—"The Rainbow Song"*

*Movement—If You Are Wearing Red*

*Puppets—Dog's Colorful Day by Emma Dodd*

*Song—"Oh, Rainbow"*

*Closing Song—"The More We Sign Together"*

*Game—Find a Color*

*Craft— "Rainbow Necklace"*

*Closing Song—"Good-bye Friends"*

## Welcome Song

Signed words are shown in italics in the song and illustrated below.

### "Hello Friends" (sung to the tune of "Goodnight Ladies")

*Hello friends, hello friends, hello friends,* we're *glad* you're here *today.*

*Hello* [each child in the class gets a turn with his or her name here], we're *glad* you're here *today.*

Hello everyone, *hello* everyone, *hello* everyone, we're *glad* you're here *today.*

**Signs:** *hello, friends, glad, today*

**Hello**

**Friends**

**Glad/Happy**

**Today**

## Theme

Introduce the theme of the day—colors. During this time, you may introduce any new signs you want them to be aware of. Start with a very simple color book—one that has just one color on each page, so that you can introduce each color's sign in addition to the color.

## Stories

**Baker, Alan.** *White Rabbit's Color Book.* **Boston: Kingfisher, 1999.**
White Rabbit wonders what it would be like to be red and jumps into the red paint. He continues to jump into yellow and blue and realizes that mixing paint makes different colors. This is a great book to teach about primary and secondary colors as well.

**Signs:** *white, red, yellow, blue, orange, purple, green, brown*

**White**

**Red**

**Yellow**

**Blue**

**Orange**

**Purple**

**Green**

**Brown**

**Cabrera, Jane.** *Cat's Colors.* **London: Puffin, 2000.**

A cute cat decides to go on a hunt to determine his favorite color.

**Signs:** *color, green, pink, black, red, yellow, purple, brown, blue, white, orange*

**Color**

**Green**

**Pink**

**Black**

**Red**

**Yellow**

**Purple**

**Brown**

**Blue**

**White**

**Orange**

**Dodd, Emma.** *Dog's Colorful Day*. **New York: Puffin, 2003.**

This story follows a white dog throughout his day. During this time, he gets into mischief and messes that leave colorful spots on him. He is then cleaned, all colors are removed, and he dreams of colorful bones.

**Signs:** *white, black, red, blue, green, brown (for chocolate), yellow, pink, gray, orange, purple*

**Optional signs:** *1–10*

**White**

**Black**

**Red**

**Blue**

**Green**

**Brown**

**Yellow**

**Pink**

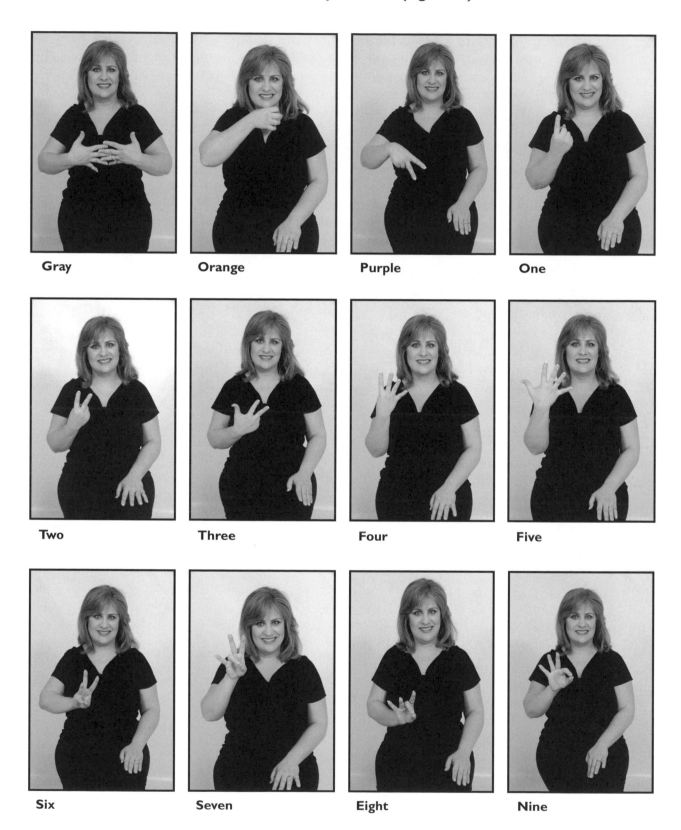

| | | | |
|---|---|---|---|
| **Gray** | **Orange** | **Purple** | **One** |
| **Two** | **Three** | **Four** | **Five** |
| **Six** | **Seven** | **Eight** | **Nine** |

**Ten**

**Fleming, Denise.** *Lunch*. **New York: Henry Holt, 1996.**

Mouse eats one colorful food after another.

**Signs:** *white, orange, yellow, green, blue, purple, red, pink, black*

**White**

**Orange**

**Yellow**

**Green**

**Blue**

**Purple**

**Red**

**Pink**

**Black**

**Lionni, Leo.** *A Color of His Own.* **New York: Knopf Books, 2006.**

A chameleon is in search of his true color. Along the way, he makes a chameleon friend and realizes that having a friend is more important than having his own color.

**Signs:** *color, green, red, gray, pink, yellow, purple, black, white*

**Color**

**Green**

**Red**

**Gray**

**Pink**

**Yellow**

**Purple**

**Black**

**White**

### "Little Boy Blue" nursery rhyme

There are many versions of this rhyme available either in alone in book format or as part of a nursery rhyme book, so I suggest using whatever copy you have available.

**Signs:** *blue, horn, sheep, cow, where, asleep*

**Blue**

**Horn**

**Sheep**

**Cow**

**Where**

**Asleep**

**Martin, Bill, Jr.** *Brown Bear, Brown Bear, What Do You See?* **New York: Henry Holt, 2008.**
Brown Bear sees a Red Bird, who sees another colored animal. This book is a great repetition story that children will love while it introduces many colors.

**Signs:** *brown, red, yellow, blue, green, purple, white, black, gold*

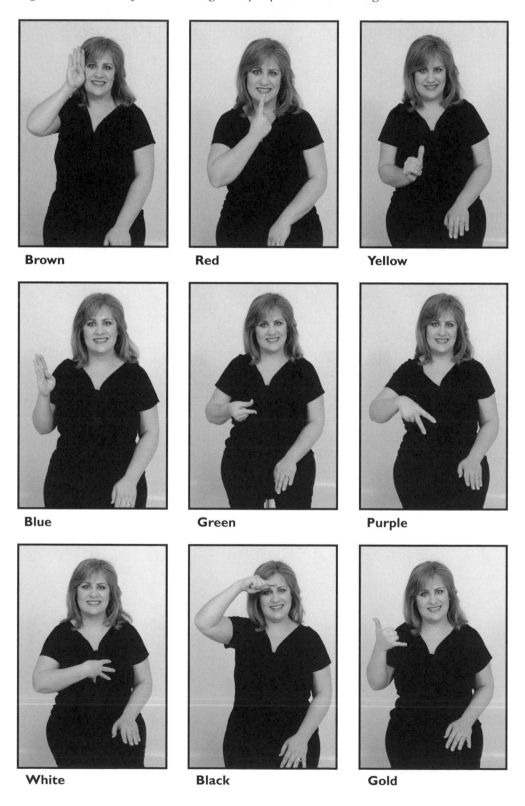

| Brown | Red | Yellow |
|-------|-----|--------|
| Blue | Green | Purple |
| White | Black | Gold |

**Milich, Zoran.** *City Colors.* **New York: Kids Can Press, 2006.**

This book leads children to discover different cities. Ten colors are featured that make learning more enjoyable and engaging for readers.

**Signs:** *red, blue, yellow, green, orange, black, white, pink, gray*

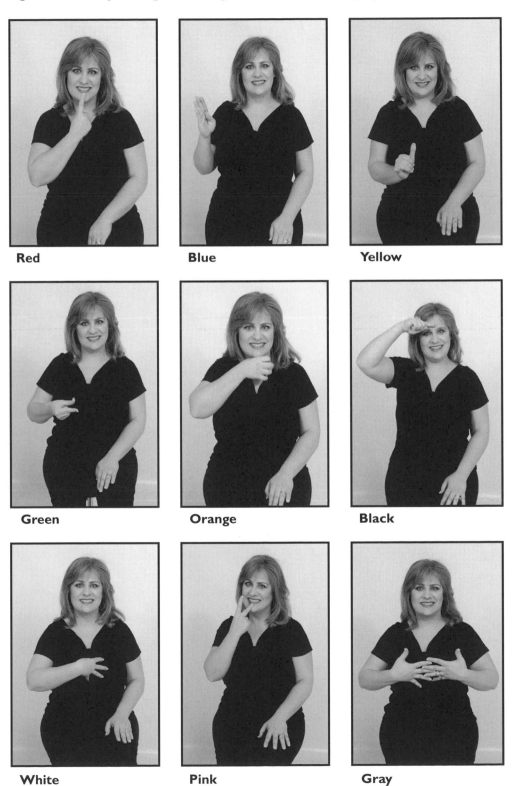

| **Red** | **Blue** | **Yellow** |
| **Green** | **Orange** | **Black** |
| **White** | **Pink** | **Gray** |

**Thong, Roseanne.** *Red Is a Dragon: A Book of Colors.* **San Francisco: Chronicle Books, 2008.**
This book uses many Asian objects (though many are universal) to help introduce many different colors.

**Signs:** *red, orange, yellow, green, blue, purple, pink, brown, white, rainbow, colors*

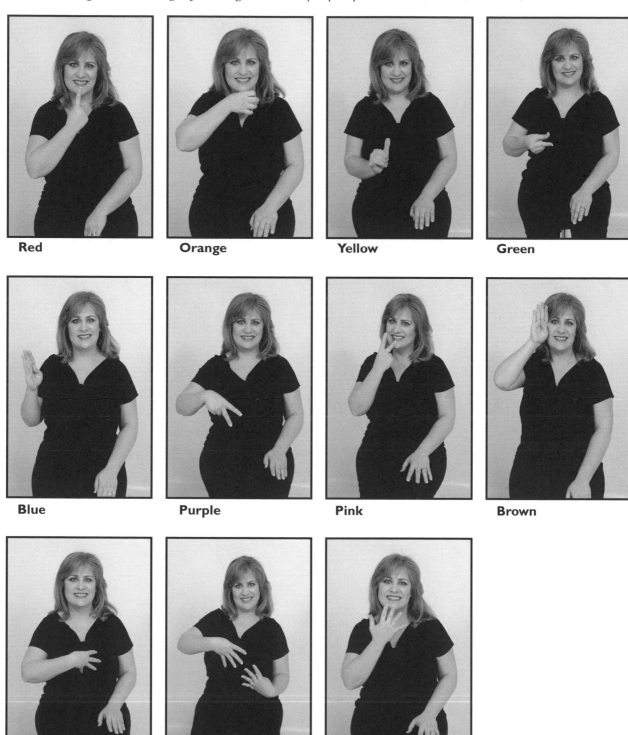

Red     Orange     Yellow     Green

Blue     Purple     Pink     Brown

White     Rainbow     Colors

**Williams, Sue.** *I Went Walking.* **New York: Live Oak Media, 2000.**

Similar in repetition to *Brown Bear, Brown Bear, What Do You See?* (see p. 156), this book is "I Went Walking, What Did I See?" The girl sees many different colors on her walk, providing a chance to engage the children while introducing them to some basic colors.

**Signs:** *black, brown, red, green, pink, yellow*

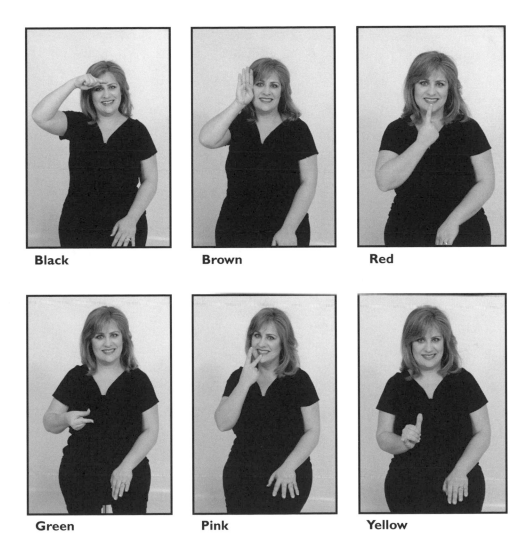

| | | |
|:---:|:---:|:---:|
| **Black** | **Brown** | **Red** |
| **Green** | **Pink** | **Yellow** |

**Wood, Jakki.** *Moo Moo, Brown Cow.* New York: Harcourt Children's Book, 1992.

Colors, numbers, and animals are all introduced in this story, as a kitten proceeds to ask each (colored) animal she finds whether or not it has any babies.

**Signs:** *brown, black, yellow, white, blue, orange, pink, green, red, rainbow*

**Optional signs:** *0–10*

**Brown**　**Black**　**Yellow**　**White**

**Blue**　**Orange**　**Pink**　**Green**

**Red**　**Rainbow**　**Zero/None**　**One**

**Two**

**Three**

**Four**

**Five**

**Six**

**Seven**

**Eight**

**Nine**

**Ten**

Yolen, Jane, and Mark Teague. *How Do Dinosaurs Learn Their Colors?* New York: Blue Sky Press, 2006.

Dinosaurs find many colored things in this fun book about colors.

**Signs:** *colors, red, purple, green, blue, pink, yellow, brown, white, black, orange, rainbows*

**Colors**

**Red**

**Purple**

**Green**

**Blue**

**Pink**

**Yellow**

**Brown**

**White**

**Black**

**Orange**

**Rainbows**

## Songs

Italicized words should be signed.

**"Oh, Rainbow." In** *Preschool Education.com: Discover the Fun in Learning.* **Preschool Education, 1997–2010. Available at www.preschooleducation.com/sallcolor.shtml. Accessed April 29, 2010.**
Sung to the tune of "Oh, Christmas Tree," this song helps children learn and sign the different colors in the rainbow.

**Signs:** *rainbow, colors, red, green, purple, orange, pink, blue*

**Rainbow**

**Colors**

**Red**

**Green**

**Purple**

**Orange**

**Pink**

**Blue**

Kidzone. "I Can Sing A Rainbow." In *Sing a Rainbow—Colourful Songs for Children Music CD.* **CYP Limited, 2010.**

**Signs:** *red, yellow, pink, green, purple, orange, blue, rainbow*

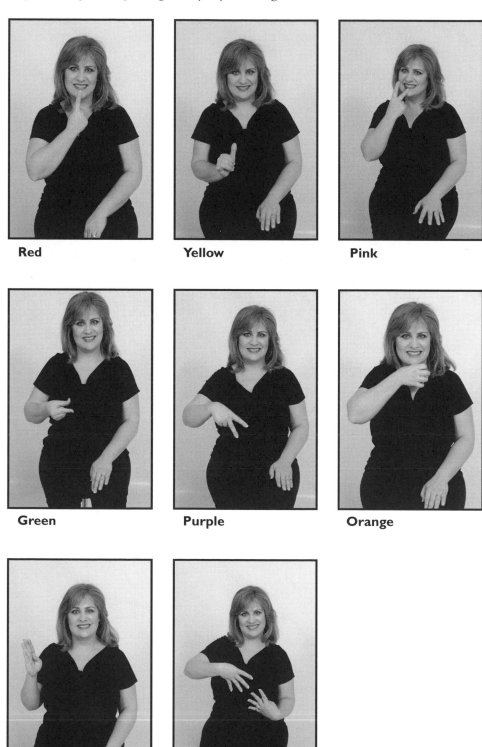

Red  Yellow  Pink

Green  Purple  Orange

Blue  Rainbow

de Azevedo Coleman, Rachel. "The Rainbow Song." In *Signing Time! Songs Vol. 4-6 Music CD*. Two Little Hands Productions, 2008.

**Signs:** *colors, rainbow, red, orange, yellow, green, purple, blue*

**Colors**

**Rainbow**

**Red**

**Orange**

**Yellow**

**Green**

**Purple**

**Blue**

de Azevedo Coleman, Rachel. "Box of Crayons." In *Signing Time! Songs Vol. 8-13 Music CD*. Two Little Hands Productions, 2008.

**Signs:** *red, orange, yellow, green, blue, pink, purple, white, color, black, brown, silver, gold*

**Optional signs:** *1, 2, 3, 4*

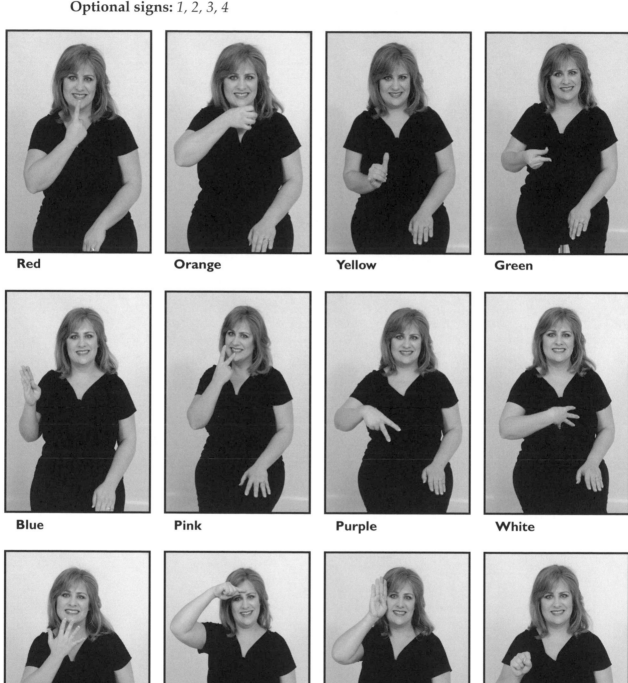

| Red | Orange | Yellow | Green |
| Blue | Pink | Purple | White |
| Color | Black | Brown | Silver |

**Gold**

## Movement

Italicized words should be signed.

**"Oh, Rainbow." In *Preschool Education.com: Discover the Fun in Learning*. Preschool Education, 1997–2010. Available at www.preschooleducation.com/sallcolor.shtml. Accessed April 29, 2010.**

This song takes the popular tune of "If You're Happy and You Know It" and changes it to "If you are wearing _____." Children look for the colors on their clothes and sign the color they are singing about. There is an action word to go along with each verse, giving children the opportunity to shake their heads, touch their shoes, pat their backs, and more. Each action word rhymes with the color mentioned in its verse. I highly recommend this one.

**Signs:** *red, blue, black, white, pink, brown, green, yellow*

**Red**

**Blue**

**Black**

**White**

| Pink | Brown | Green | Yellow |

### Make a Rainbow

Give each child a color to find and have him or her collect things from around the room of that color. Use the items to create a large rainbow on the floor.

### Find a Color

Make color circles ahead of time using crayons or markers to color in the shape on pieces of paper. They should be about 12 inches in diameter, and whatever shape you want to make them is fine. Scatter the color circles around the room on the floor. Ask the children to go stand on the color red (say it and sign it). Children then find that color and stand on the circle. Call out another color and sign it. Children again find the color and stand on it. After you have called out all of the colors and the children have found all of them, try silent play. Don't say the word, just sign it. Children still look for and stand on the color when they find it, but with everyone signing only. (A variation of this game is to use the big color circles to play a concentration game. Children need to sign the color when they flip it over.)

## Puppets

### Dodd, Emma. *Dog's Colorful Day*. New York: Puffin, 2003.

Use a white dog puppet or stuffed animal to act out *Dog's Colorful Day*. Make colored dots ahead of time on paper and put little pieces of tape on the back so that they'll stick to the puppet. As the dog gets another spot on him on the story, put that color spot on the white dog puppet. (You may have the children add the dots—they like that!) Everyone signs the color as it gets put on the dog. When dog takes his bath at the end, rub off all the colored dots.

## Activities/Games/Props

### Who Has the Block?

Use a wooden or plastic block, or any other object that is a solid color. Have all of the children hide their eyes and give the block to one child to hide. Have the children open their eyes and try to guess which child is holding the block. After they discover who has it, ask the child what color it is and to sign it for the group. Then have all of the children say it and sign it. Do this activity again, but give a different child a different color block. Keep going until you've had a chance for everyone to hide the block from their classmates and have used every color block you have.

A variation of this would be that after you hide the block, begin singing a revised version of the song "Who Has the Frog?" by Rachel de Azevedo Coleman, from *Signing Time, Series 2 Volumes 8–13 Music CD* (Two Little Hands Productions, 2008).

*Who, who, who* has the block?
*Where, where, where* did it go?
*How, how, how* did we lose it?
Where'd it go? Where'd it go?

**Signs:** *who, where, how*

**Who**     **Where**     **How**

### Red Light, Green Light

Children stand in a line away from you and you sign red light for them to stop and green light for them to go (meaning take a step toward you). Take turns going back and forth from green to red. Whoever touches you first wins and gets to be the caller (the one who signs red light or green light).

**Signs:** *red, green*

**Red**         **Green**

## Crafts

"Rainbow Necklace." In *Preschool Education.com: Discover the Fun in Learning.* Preschool Education, 1997–2010. Available at www.preschooleducation.com/aallcolor.shtml. Accessed April 29, 2010.

**NOTE:** *Check for any food allergies in the class first, before doing this activity.*

Children make colored necklaces using colored cereal. You may have the children sort the colors before they make their necklaces by putting each color in its own bowl or baggie. You may even sort and put one color in the baggie, crush them, and then add another color and crush them up. See what your baggies look like after adding several colors—did you make a rainbow colored powder? ("Fruit Loop Color," *Everything Preschool* www.everythingpreschool.com/themes/colors/art.htm). For another variation of this activity, make a rainbow with your cereal by gluing the pieces in the shape of a rainbow on white paper ( "Fruit Loop Rainbow," *Everything Preschool,*www. everythingpreschool.com/themes/colors/art.htm).

"Tie Die Sheet." In *Everything Preschool.* **Available at www.everythingpreschool.com/ themes/colors/art.htm. Accessed April 29, 2010.**

Participants in your storytime will LOVE this activity. With paint put in spray bottles, they get to spray a large white sheet, filling it up with all of the different colors in the rainbow. When the sheet is completely dry, the children will have created a beautiful, colorful mural that you may hang in your storytime room.

### Rainbow Handprints

**Materials Needed:** large white construction paper (18-by-12-inch works well), nontoxic washable paint or finger paints, water, wipes for hands

**Directions:** Give the children a piece of paper and have them dip either their hands or their fingers into the paint and use them to make a rainbow on their paper. Wipe little hands clean immediately.

## Closing Songs

Italicized words should be signed.

### "The More We Sign Together"
### (Sing to the tune of "The More We Get Together.")

The *more* we *sign together, together, together,*

The *more* we *sign together,* the *happier* we'll be.

For *your friends* are *my friends* and *my friends* are *your friends,*

The *more* we *sign together* the *happier* we'll be.

**Signs:** *more, sign, together, happy, yours, friends, my*

| More | Sign | Together | Happy |

**Yours**

**Friends**

**My**

"Good-bye Friends"
(Sing to the tune of "Goodnight Ladies.")

*Good-bye friends, good-bye friends, good-bye friends,* we'll *see you* here *again.*

*Good-bye* [each child in the class gets a turn with his or her name here], we'll *see you* here *again.*

*Good-bye everyone, good-bye everyone, good-bye everyone,* we'll *see you* here *again.*

**Signs:** *good-bye, friends, see you, again*

**Good-bye**

**Friends**

**See You**

**Again**

The children in your storytime have now been able to experience the colors in many different ways: through hearing, seeing, saying, signing, singing, doing, and creating. As a result, they will remember their colors much more easily. You have also made learning colors a whole lot of fun! The next chapter takes a look at one more theme—farm animals. Just about all children absolutely LOVE animals, so it is a great storytime topic.

# Glossary of Signs Used in Color Theme

**Again**

**Asleep**

**Black**

**Blue**

**Brown**

**Color**

**Cow**

**Eight**

**Five**

**Four**

**Friends**

**Glad/Happy**

# Glossary of Signs Used in Color Theme

Gold     Good-bye     Gray     Green

Hello     Horn     How     More

My     Nine     One     Orange

# Glossary of Signs Used in Color Theme

**Pink**

**Purple**

**Rainbow**

**Red**

**See**

**See You**

**Seven**

**Sheep**

**Sign**

**Six**

**Ten**

**Three**

# Glossary of Signs Used in Color Theme

**Today**

**Together**

**Two**

**Where**

**White**

**Who**

**Yellow**

**You**

**Yours**

**Zero/None**

# Chapter 10

# Farm Animals Storytime with Sign Language

> **Signing Tip**: Did you know that many sign language signs are iconic in nature— meaning that the sign often looks like the actual object? This helps children learn and remember the meaning of new words much more easily. For example, when you make the sign for tiger, you show the stripes on your face, and for the sign for kangaroo you make its paws in front of you and pretend to hop. With many of the animal signs in particular, children get the chance to act just like the animal, while also using sign language.

Young children enjoy seeing and learning about animals, so farm animals is a great theme to incorporate into your storytime. Children will become even more engaged when they get the opportunity to act like the animals through the signs and to interact with one another through games and activities.

## Sample Lesson Plan for a 45-Minute Lesson

Again, if you wish, substitute books, songs, and activities you are comfortable with for those listed here.

*Welcome Song—"Hello Friends"*

*Book—*The Cow Who Clucked *by Denise Fleming*

*Song—"Old Macdonald Had a Farm"*

*Movement—"Horse Goes Over the Jump"*

*Book—*Duck on a Bike *by David Shannon*

*Flannel Board—Counting Cats*

*Movement—"Chicken Dance"*

*Closing Song—"The More We Sign Together"*

*Game—Dog, Dog, Cat*

*Craft—"Tire Track Art"*

*Closing Song—"Good-bye Friends"*

## Welcome Song

Signed words are shown in italics in the song and illustrated below.

### "Hello Friends" (Sing to the tune of "Goodnight Ladies.")

*Hello friends, hello friends, hello friends*, we're *glad* you're here *today*.

*Hello* [each child in the class gets a turn with his or her name here], we're *glad* you're here *today*.

Hello everyone, *hello* everyone, *hello* everyone, we're *glad* you're here *today*.

**Signs:** *hello, friends, glad, today*

**Hello**

**Friends**

**Glad/Happy**

**Today**

## Theme

Introduce the theme of the day—farm animals. You may want to begin your storytime by talking about the animals that the children already know live on a farm. You can then show them the signs for the animals as they are discussed.

## Stories

**Boynton, Sandra. *Barnyard Dance.* New York: Workman Publishing, 1993.**
The animals on the farm have a fun hoe-down barnyard dance.

**Signs:** *horse, cow, pig, bunny, duck, chicken, mouse (mice), donkey, sheep, turkey, frog, dog*

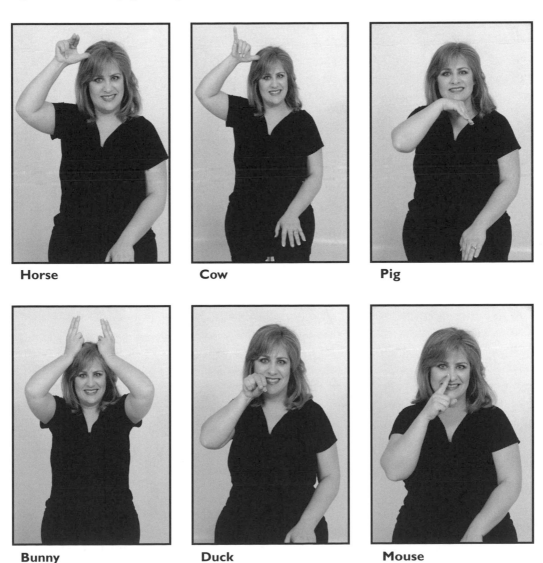

| **Horse** | **Cow** | **Pig** |

| **Bunny** | **Duck** | **Mouse** |

**Chicken**

**Donkey**

**Sheep**

**Turkey**

**Frog**

**Dog**

Bruss, Deborah. *Book, Book, Book.* New York: Arthur A. Levine Books, 2001.

When the children go back to school in the fall, the farm animals are bored. They search for something to do and find their local library.

**Signs:** *farm, horse, cow, goat, pig, duck, hen*

**Farm**

**Horse**

**Cow**

**Goat**

**Pig**

**Duck**

**Chicken**

**Hen (sign H-E-N or sign Chicken)**

**Clarke, Gus.** *EIEIO: The Story of Old MacDonald, Who Had a Farm.* **New York: Lothrop, Lee & Shepard, 1992.**

This book begins just like the song we all know and enjoy, but has a twist for an ending when Old MacDonald has had enough with hearing all of the animals' noises.

**Signs:** *farm, duck, pig, cow, hen, sheep, geese, dog*

**Farm**

**Duck**

**Pig**

**Cow**

**Hen (sign H-E-N or sign Chicken)**                **Sheep**

**Chicken**                **Geese**                **Dog**

Clarke, Jane. *Stuck in the Mud*. New York: Walker Books, 2008.

Hen discovers that one of her chicks is stuck in the mud. The farm animals each try to get the baby chick unstuck.

**Signs:** *hen, chick, cat, dog, sheep, horse, farmer*

**Hen (sign H-E-N or sign Chicken)**                **Cat**

**Chicken/Chick**

**Dog**

**Sheep**

**Horse**

**Farmer (sign Farm and Person)**

**Cronin, Doreen.** *Click, Clack, Moo: Cows That Type.* **New York: Simon & Schuster, 2000.**
The cows and hen negotiate with Farmer Brown to get what they want.

**Signs:** *cow, hen, farmer, duck*

**Cow**

**Hen (sign H-E-N or sign Chicken)**

**Chicken**

**Farmer (sign Farm and Person)**

**Duck**

Edwards, Pamela Duncan. *The Grumpy Morning*. New York: Hyperion Books for Children, 1998.

What happens on the farm when the farmer sleeps late? A grumpy morning for the farm animals.

**Signs:** *cow, dog, goat, hog, rabbit, horse, duck, cat, owl, hen, moth, farmer*

**Cow**          **Dog**          **Goat**          **Hog/Pig**

**Rabbit**

**Horse**

**Duck**

**Cat**

**Owl**

**Hen (Sign H-E-N or sign Chicken)**

**Chicken**

**Farmer (sign Farm and Person)**

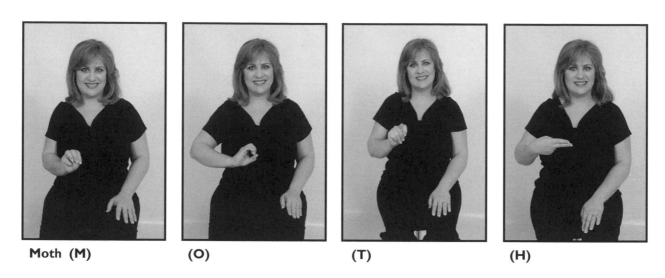

**Moth  (M)**        **(O)**        **(T)**        **(H)**

**Fleming, Denise.** *The Cow Who Clucked.* **New York: Henry Holt, 2006.**
Cow has lost her moo. Which animal on the farm has it?

**Signs:** *cow, dog, bee, cat, fish, duck, goat, mouse, snake, owl, squirrel, hen*

**Cow**        **Dog**        **Bee**        **Cat**

**Fish**        **Duck**        **Goat**        **Mouse**

**Snake**

**Owl**

**Squirrel**

**Hen (sign H-E-N or sign Chicken)**

**Chicken**

**Kutner, Merrily.** *Down on the Farm.* **New York: Holiday House, 2005.**

A great book to introduce the animals on the farm and the sounds they make.

**Signs:** *farm, rooster, crow (bird), horse, cow, duck, geese, turkey, dog, pig, goat, sheep, chick (chicken), cat*

**Farm**

**Rooster**

**Bird**

**Horse**

**Crows (Sign C-R-O-W or sign Bird)**

**Cow**

**Duck**

**Geese**

**Turkey**

**Dog**

**Pig**

**Goat**

**Sheep**

**Chicken/Chicks**

**Cat**

**Shannon, David.** *Duck on a Bike.* **New York: Blue Sky Press, 2002.**

Duck decides to try riding a bike. As he rides by the farm animals, each has a thought to share about duck's idea of riding a bike.

**Signs:** *duck, cow, sheep, dog, cat, horse, chicken, goat, pig, mouse, animals*

**Duck**

**Cow**

**Sheep**

**Dog**

Cat

Horse

Chicken/Chicks

Goat

Pig

Mouse

Animals

**Williams, Sue.** *Let's Go Visiting.* **New York: Harcourt Brace, 1998.**

> A child visits some baby farm animals to see who is ready to play.

> **Signs:** *baby, foal, calves, kittens, piglets, ducklings, puppies*

> **Optional signs:** *numbers 1–6*

Baby

Foal/Horse

Calves/Cow

Kittens/Cat

**Piglets/Pig**

**Ducklings/Duck**

**Puppies/Dog**

**One**

**Two**

**Three**

**Four**

**Five**

**Six**

## Songs

Italicized words should be signed.

### "Old McDonald Had a Farm"

Old Macdonald had a *farm*, E-I-E-I-O,
And on his *farm* he had a *cow*,
E-I-E-I-O.With a moo-moo here and a moo-moo there [continue to sign cow while saying moo],
Here a moo, there a moo,
Everywhere a moo-moo.
Old Macdonald had a *farm*, E-I-E-I-O.

Old Macdonald had a *farm*, E-I-E-I-O,
And on his *farm* he had a *pig*, E-I-E-I-O.
With a (snort) here and a (snort) there [continue to sign pig while snorting],
Here a (snort), there a (snort),
Everywhere a (snort-snort).
Old Macdonald had a *farm*, E-I-E-I-O.

Old Macdonald had a *farm*, E-I-E-I-O,
And on his *farm* he had a *horse*, E-I-E-I-O
With a neigh, neigh here and a neigh, neigh there [continue to sign horse],
Here a neigh, there a neigh,
Everywhere a neigh, neigh.

Old Macdonald had a *farm*, E-I-E-I-O.
Old Macdonald had a *farm*, E-I-E-I-O,
And on his *farm* he had a *chicken*, E-I-E-I-O.
With a cluck, cluck here and a cluck, cluck there [continue to sign chicken],
Here a cluck, there a cluck,
Everywhere a cluck, cluck

Old Macdonald had a *farm*, E-I-E-I-O.
Old Macdonald had a *farm*, E-I-E-I-O,
And on his farm he had a *duck*,
E-I-E-I-O.With a quack, quack here and a quack, quack there [continue to sign duck],
Here a quack, there a quack,
Everywhere a quack, quack.
Old Macdonald had a *farm*, E-I-E-I-O.

Continue adding animals with their sounds. You may also let the children pick the next farm animal/sound to sing.

**Signs:** *farm, cow, pig, horse, chicken, duck*

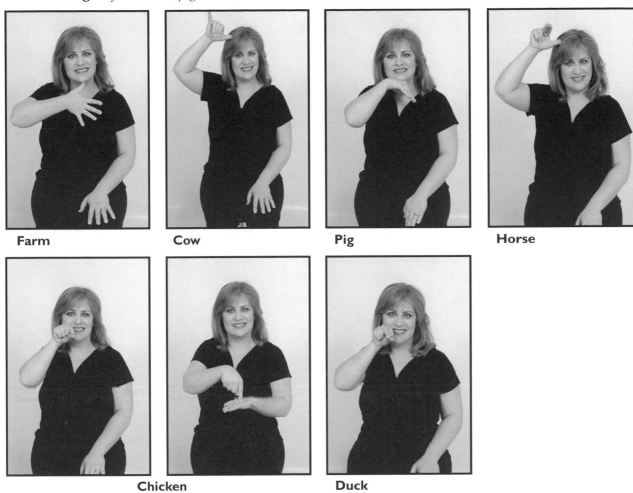

**Farm**  **Cow**  **Pig**  **Horse**

**Chicken**  **Duck**

de Azevedo Coleman, Rachel. "Leah's Farm." In *Signing Time! Songs Vols. 7–9 Music CD.* Two Little Hands Productions, 2008.

**Signs:** *farm, chicken, horse, goat, mouse, rooster, sheep, cow, donkey, pig, turkey*

**Farm**  **Chicken**  **Horse**

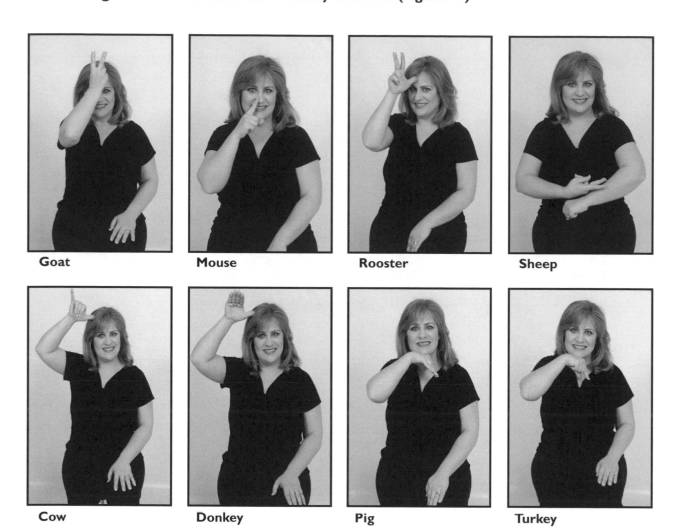

Goat     Mouse     Rooster     Sheep

Cow     Donkey     Pig     Turkey

**"Animal Sounds."** In *Preschool Education.* **Available at www.preschooleducation.com/ sfarm.shtml. Accessed April 29, 2010.**

Sung to the tune of the "Wheels on the Bus," in this song the animals on the farm make their animal sounds. You may sing the verses with any farm animal you want, so use the sign glossary at the end of this chapter to find the signs you'd like to use for this song.

### "If I Were a Farmer" (Sing to "Did You Ever See a Lassie?")

Oh, if I were a *farmer*, a *farmer*, a *farmer*,
Oh, if I were a *farmer*, what would I do?
I would milk the *cows* each *day*, Each *day*, each *day*.
I would milk the *cows* each *day*, that's what I'd do.

Oh, if I were a *farmer*, a *farmer*, a *farmer*,
Oh, if I were a *farmer*, what would I do?
I would feed the *horses* hay,
Each *day*, each *day*.
I would feed the *horses* hay, that's what I'd do.

Oh, if I were a *farmer*, a *farmer*, *a farmer*,
Oh, if I were a *farmer*, what would I do?
I would gather eggs from the *chickens*,
Each *day*, each *day*.
I would gather eggs from the *chickens*, that's what I'd do.

Oh, if I were a *farmer*, a *farmer*, *a farmer*,
Oh, if I were a *farmer*, what would I do?
I would shear the *sheep* each *day*,
Each *day*, each *day*.
I would shear the *sheep* each *day*, that's what I'd do.

You can continue this song by substituting each animal on the farm and something you would do with that animal (give the cats milk, chase the mice away, wake up to the rooster, etc.)

**Signs:** *farmer, cows, day, horses, chickens, sheep*

**Farmer**    **Cows**    **Day**

**Horses**    **Chickens**    **Sheep**

## Movement

### Charades
Children may take turns acting like different farm animals and letting the others in the storytime guess and sign their animal.

**DJ's Choice. "Chicken Dance." In** *DJ's Choice (Kids Fun: Games, Songs & Sing-A-Longs Music CD*. **DJ's Choice, 1998.**
Play the music and have the children do the classic dance. For a signing twist, sign *chicken* along with the dance by signing the first part of the sign "beak, beak, beak, beak," the second part of the sign "hand, hand, hand, hand," then finish the classic way "wiggle, wiggle, wiggle, wiggle" "clap, clap, clap, clap".

**Signs:** *chicken*

**Chicken**

### "Horse Goes Over the Jump"
### (Sing to the Tune of "Here We Go Round the Mulberry Bush.")
The *horse* likes to go over the jump, over the jump, over the jump.
The *horse* likes to go over the jump, all around the *farm*.

The *pigs* like to roll in the mud, roll in the mud, roll in the mud.
The *pigs* like to roll in the mud, all around the *farm*.

The *ducks* like to waddle around, waddle around, waddle around.
The *ducks* like to waddle around, all around the *farm*.

The *rooster* likes to strut his stuff, strut his stuff, strut his stuff.
The *rooster* likes to strut his stuff, all around the *farm*.

The *cows* like to eat the grass, eat the grass, eat the grass.
The *cows* like to eat the grass, all around the *farm*.

The *chickens* like to peck the ground, peck the ground, peck the ground.
The *chickens* like to peck the ground, all around the *farm*.

The *dogs* like to chase the *sheep*, chase the *sheep*, chase the *sheep*.
The *dogs* like to chase the *sheep*, all around the *farm*.

The *cats* like to lick their paws, lick their paws, lick their paws.
The *cats* like to lick their paws, all around the *farm*.

Children may sign each animal and then act like the animal on the farm with the action the song tells them to do.

**Signs:** *horse, farm, pigs, ducks, rooster, cows, chicken, dogs, sheep, cats*

**Horse**          **Farm**          **Pigs**          **Ducks**

**Rooster**          **Cows**          **Chicken**

**Dogs**

**Sheep**

**Cats**

## Flannel Board

"Counting Cats" (Sing to "Ten Little Indians.")

One little, two little, three little *cats*,
Four little, five little, six little *cats*,
Seven little, eight little, nine little *cats*,
Ten are in the barn.
All are white with ears black,
Fluffy tails all in black,
Hold them, pet them, put them back,
Ten are in the barn.
One little, two little, three little *cats*,
Four little, five little, six little *cats*,
Seven little, eight little, nine little *cats*,
Ten are in the barn.

This is a great song to do along with a flannel board. Cut 10 cat shapes out of white felt and a big barn out of brown felt. Place the barn shape on a flannel board. As you sing the first verse, place the cat shapes by the barn, one at a time. Then remove the cats as you sing the last verse.

If you have enough felt, replace the word *cats* with different farm animals and do the song over and over again for each farm animal (cutting out the middle verse). You may also substitute the last line for where the animal is, like ducks in the pond or horses in the field. Of course you could always add the sound that the animal makes at the end of each line for extra fun.

**Signs:** *cats*

**Cats**

## Activities/Games/Props

### Dog, Dog, Cat

Similar to Duck, Duck, Goose, but the children have to sign it and not say it (making it a quieter version of this game). As they tap each child with one hand when they walk around the circle, they sign the farm animal with their other hand. You don't have to use *dog* and *cat*; you may use whatever farm animals you want (as long as the sign doesn't require two hands.)

**Signs:** *dog, cat*

**Dog**          **Cat**

### Animal Alphabet Match-Up Puzzle

You can purchase this puzzle from Garlic Press, Harris Communications, and many other locations. If you go online and search for the title as shown you will find many stores that offer it. This puzzle has the picture of the animal on one card and the ASL sign for the animal on another card. Children find the two cards that match and put them together. Although these puzzles aren't specific to farm animals, they are a fun way to practice animal recognition and signs.

### Who Has the Horse?

Use a plastic figurine of any farm animal. Have all the children hide their eyes and then give the item(s) to one child to hide. Have the children then open their eyes and try to guess which child is holding the farm animal. After they discover who has it, ask the child what animal it is and to sign it for the group. Then have all the children say it and sign it. Do this activity again, but give a different child a different animal. Keep going until everyone has had a chance to hide the animal from the storytime class.

A variation of this game may be played if you only have one animal. Play the game like hot potato. Pass the animal around to music ("Leah's Farm," mentioned in the song section of this chapter, would be a good one, but any farm-sounding hoe-down song will work). Whoever is holding the animal when the music stops has to sign it for the rest of the storytime group. Keep going until everyone has had a turn.

## Crafts

### Woolly Sheep

**Materials Needed:** cut-out pictures of sheep, one for each child (there is a sheep template in the appendix); two bags of cotton balls; all-purpose or craft nontoxic glue

**Directions:** Children put a drop of glue on each piece of cotton and glue it onto the sheep (making it into a woolly sheep).

**"Hand Horses."** In *Preschool Education.com: Discover the Fun in Learning.* **Preschool Education, 1997–2010. Available at www.preschooleducation.com/afarm.shtml. Accessed April 29, 2010.**

Children's hands are used to create a handprint horse. See the photo of one I made below.

**Handprint Horse**

**"Tire Track Art."** In *Everything Preschool.* **Available at www.everythingpreschool.com/themes/transportation/art.htm. Accessed April 29, 2010.**

Although this calls for a variety of vehicles, I would use only toy tractors, if you have enough of them. Children dip their toy tractors in the paint and make trails. Fun!

## Closing Songs

Italicized words should be signed.

**"The More We Sign Together"**
**(Sing to the tune of "The More We Get Together.")**

The *more* we *sign together, together, together,*
The *more* we *sign together,* the *happier* we'll be.
For *your friends* are *my friends* and *my friends* are *your friends,*
The *more* we *sign together* the *happier* we'll be.

**Signs:** *more, sign, together, happy, your, friends, my*

**More**

**Sign**

**Together**

**Happy**

**Your**

**Friends**

**My**

"Good-bye Friends"
(Sing to the tune of "Goodnight Ladies.")

*Good-bye friends, good-bye friends, good-bye friends,* we'll *see you* here *again.*

*Good-bye* [each child in the class gets a turn with his or her name here], we'll *see you* here *again.*

*Good-bye* everyone, *good-bye* everyone, *good-bye* everyone, we'll *see you* here *again.*

**Signs:** *good-bye, friends, see you, again*

**Good-bye**  **Friends**  **See You**  **Again**

Animals are a fun topic for children as well as adults. Because many of the signs look like aspects of each animal, children can act like the animal through their signs and enjoy learning about farm animals that much more. Through the fun hoe-down songs, stories, and activities and crafts, participants in your signing storytime will have a really enjoyable time. The last few chapters have shown how to include sign language into your storytime program, as well as providing a few samples of new programs you can try. You have learned how to incorporate sign language into your baby, toddler, preschool, and primary age children's programs. The next chapter moves on to the last age group of children in your Library—'tweens and teens.

# Glossary of Signs Used in Farm Animal Theme

**Again**

**Animals**

**Bee**

**Bunny/Rabbit**

**Cat**

**Chicken**

**Clean**

**Crow (C)**

**(R)**

**(O)**

**(W)**

# Glossary of Signs Used in Farm Animal Theme

**Cow**

**Dog**

**Donkey**

**Duck**

**Eight**

**Farm**

**Farmer (Farm + Person)**

**Fish**

**Five**

**Friend**

**Four**

# Glossary of Signs Used in Farm Animal Theme

**Frog**

**Geese**

**Glad/Happy**

**Goat**

**Good-bye**

**Hello**

**Hog/Pig**

**Horse**

**More**

**Morning**

**Mouse**

**My**

# Glossary of Signs Used in Farm Animal Theme

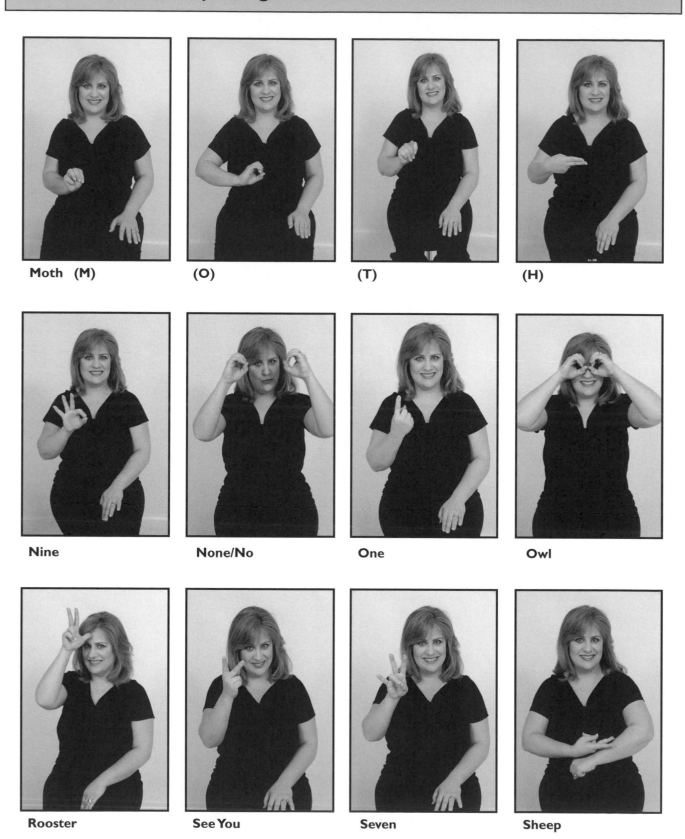

Moth (M)

(O)

(T)

(H)

Nine

None/No

One

Owl

Rooster

See You

Seven

Sheep

# Glossary of Signs Used in Farm Animal Theme

**Sign**

**Six**

**Snake**

**Squirrel**

**Ten**

**Three**

**Today**

**Together**

**Turkey**

**Two**

# Part IV

Programs for 'Tweens and Teens
(Ages 8 and Up)

# Chapter 11

# Working with 'Tweens and Teens

Please keep in mind that in this and the following chapter, I may be stretching the term *'tween* a little bit to include eight- and nine-year-olds. However, the tips and programs I'm suggesting work well for that age group as well as for your teens.

Chapter 12 provides examples of great new programs that incorporate sign language. If you already offer one or two of the following programs, you'll be able to see how, by just tweaking them a little bit, you can add some ASL signs to give them a new twist. If particular signs are suggested for a program, you'll see what words to sign and how to make the sign as well.

Following are some steps to keep in mind when working with the 'tween and teen age group that will make incorporating sign language into your programs much easier.

## 1. Get Them to Sign Up!

'Tweens and teens don't have to bring their parents with them to your library because they are gaining more independence. In addition, their parents aren't necessarily signing them up for the programs you offer. 'Tweens and teens are given more choice of what types of programs interest them and that they choose to participate in. Your job will be getting them interested enough to sign up and want to participate in your sign language programs.

Promotional information about the programs should be published in your library newsletter and any other typical medium that you use to promote your programs. I also recommend sharing your program information with any writing, drama, ASL, or game clubs/courses that are held at your local middle and high schools, as those clubs and classes are most suited to the program suggestions offered in the next chapter. Many of the programs may easily include hearing impaired 'tweens and teens, so you'll want to publicize your programs to any hearing impaired or deaf clubs in your community as well.

## 2. Have Your Resources Ready and Available!

Most likely, 'tweens and teens will be signing up for your programs because they are interested in learning more about sign language, and in your programs they will be learning some signs. You should have a display of your ASL materials for participants to peruse and reference before, during, and after your programs that incorporate sign language. Participants will need to look up signs and information in your available materials, and since they are interested in your topic, they will most likely be interested in borrowing the materials when your program is concluded.

Don't forget to use the resources that appear in the back of this book and let participants know about the online dictionaries that are available. The suggested resources can help you make sure you are teaching each ASL sign correctly and that your participants are staying true to the language.

## 3. Stay as True to the Language as You Can!

Don't forget to explain to the 'tweens and teens that they will be learning signs from an actual language, ASL. To remain respectful of that language, it is important to stay as true to it as you can. If using a sign, it is important that participants don't make up a gesture, but use the resources available to them in print and online to look up the actual sign so that they are as accurate as possible.

As discussed previously, you'll also want to explain to participants that just as many language have variations in words used (soda vs. pop) or accents used in various parts of a country, ASL has variation as well. Although the resources are wonderful, people in your location may make that particular sign a little bit differently. That's okay. Your program may use signs previously learned from a deaf neighbor or family member, from the resources you have, or, if you choose to have a Certified American Sign Language Interpreter come to assist in teaching some signs to the participants, that's okay, too!

## 4. Make it F-U-N!

When publicizing your programs, and then throughout the programs, make them as fun as possible. Your participants already have some interest in learning some sign language or just really like the idea of participating in the type of program you are offering. Making the program as fun as possible while the participants are there at your library is a surefire way to get them borrowing your materials and coming back to participate in other programs. They may also be able to offer suggestions for other programs they'd love to be a part of, giving you ideas for future programs. The more fun you have with these programs, the more fun your participants will have. They'll spread the word to their friends and come back again and again for more fun programming at your library.

These tips will help to make your 'tween and teen programs a success. If you keep in mind the various ways to get potential participants interested in the programs; keep your resources ready and available during the programs; and most important, keep your programs fun, participants will have an enjoyable time at your library and will want to come back for more (and bring their friends with them the next time). The next chapter provides some really FUN programs that include ASL signs to offer your 'tween and teen community.

# Program Ideas for Elementary/'Tweens/Teens

Library programs that incorporate ASL are not just for babies, toddlers, and preschoolers. Elementary age children, 'tweens, and teens in your program can also have a lot of fun with new programs that incorporate sign language. For the program ideas throughout this chapter, you'll find a suggested age group, materials needed, approximate length of time, and directions for running the program: again, everything you need to get started incorporating the programs into your library. Pick and choose those that appeal to you the most, that you are the most comfortable promoting and teaching, and that you think will appeal the most to your library population.

The first four game suggestions may be offered each as its own program or be combined to make a four-week (meeting once a week) Sign Language Game Club. Each game could be played a different week within the time period, offering the children the opportunity to play several different games in sign language.

**Silent Red Light, Green Light**

> **Age Group:** intermediate elementary (ages 8–10), maybe also into the 'tweens
>
> **Estimated Time:** 45 minutes to 1 hour
>
> **Materials Needed:** room to run (a great activity to offer outdoors)
>
> **Directions:** Start by introducing the program participants to ASL, why we have ASL (a way to communicate for those who are hearing impaired or deaf) and what it is used for (hearing impaired and deaf people to communicate with each other and with hearing people who know the language, as well as more recently to help babies communicate before they can speak and to help young children learn).

Explain that you will be revising the traditional game Red Light, Green Light as they know it and making it into a silent game using sign language only. You may want to specifically invite hearing impaired children from your community to play and participate in this program with the hearing children, as this is a game they could also play because there will be no voices used and signs will be the only method of communication.

Choose one person to be the caller. The caller is to stand with his or her face toward the rest of the players, who will be quite a distance away in a horizontal line so that each player is about the same distance away from the caller. (In the traditional game, the caller's back is toward the other players, but because this is a sign language game, the players have to be able to see the caller.)

The caller will face the players with his or her eyes closed, so as not to see how close the players are getting (you may want to use a blindfold to prevent cheating). The caller will sign *red light* to make the other players stop taking steps toward him or her. The caller will sign *green light* to allow the other players to take steps, keeping his or her eyes closed. The object of the game is for the first player who can reach the caller to touch him or her, letting them know that they are caught. That player then becomes the caller.

**Signs:** *red, green, light*

**Red**       **Green**       **Light**

**Silent Hangman**

**Age Group:** elementary (ages 8–10), 'tweens

**Estimated Time:** 1 hour

**Materials Needed:** blackboard, whiteboard, or large chart paper to make the hangman; writing tool that works on the boards or paper; poster or handouts of the manual alphabet for participants to refer to (see handout in the appendix)

**Directions:** Just as in the regular game of Hangman, one person will be the leader—the person who makes up the word and puts the number of dashes down to show how many letters are in the word chosen. The leader will also draw the hangman as each letter is suggested (if it is wrong, of course). The difference between our silent hangman and regular hangman is that silent hangman is a silent game.

To guess the letters, players have to show the leader the letter using their hands, using the manual alphabet. The leader will sign back *yes* if the guess is correct and place the letter in the correct dash where the letter belongs in the word. If the letter is incorrect, the leader will sign back *no* and draw a part of the hangman. The leader may then select another player by pointing to someone. Again, the player will show the leader his or her guess by showing the leader the manual alphabet letter, and the leader will sign back *yes* or *no*. When someone has a guess for the entire word, he or she will fingerspell it using the manual alphabet, instead of calling out the word.

This is another program that is great to reach out to the hearing impaired community, because hearing impaired and hearing children can play this game together with no voices used—only sign language.

**Signs:** *manual alphabet (see the appendix), yes, no*

Yes        No

### Fingerspelling Bingo

**Age Group:** elementary (ages 8–10), 'tweens, teens

**Estimated Time:** 1 hour

**Materials Needed:** bingo cards with the letters of the alphabet (not the manual alphabet, the regular alphabet, and each in a different place on the card, not every letter on every card), poster or handouts of the manual alphabet so that players can refer to it (see handout in the appendix, or buy them by searching online for "American Sign Language alphabet poster"; several companies offer them), chips or little pieces of paper for the players to cover up the letters on their bingo cards, piece of paper, pen/pencil

To make the materials easier for this game, you may want to look for a manual alphabet game that has already been developed, such as Finger Alphabet Lotto or ASLingo (both available for purchase at ADCO Hearing Products or Harris Communications, listed in the resources section). They may also be available at other stores that carry ASL products and games.

**Directions:** This game is also played silently, offering a great opportunity to invite the hearing impaired community to play along with the hearing community in your library. Every player, except for the caller, begins with a bingo card and a little pile of chips or pieces of paper. The caller shows the players a manual alphabet letter. If they have that letter on their card, they will cover it with a chip/paper. If they don't have that letter, they don't do anything. The caller has to keep track of which letters have been shown, writing down each on the piece of paper so that only the caller can refer to it if needed. The caller continues to show the players manual letters, and the players continue to cover the letters on their bingo cards if they match the manual letter shown. Once a player has filled his or her card (or gotten one row or column filled—this playing option is up to you), that player wins the game. This game may be played over again several times. It is your decision whether to offer a prize or reward to the winner of each game, give every player a prize at the end, or not offer any prizes at all (just the reward of having won).

## Sign Language Charades

**Age Group:** elementary (8–10), 'tweens, teens

**Estimated Time:** 1 hour

**Materials Needed:** none, though you'll probably want a computer close by with an online ASL dictionary or a hard copy ASL dictionary available for the leaders to refer to

**Directions:** In regular charades, the leader wants the players to guess a word and provides clues in the form of gestures to get the players to guess the word with no voice used by the leader. This game works similarly, as the leader has a word for the players to try to guess and can't use his or her voice, but instead of using gestures, the leader makes the sign language signs for each word. The players closely watch the leader make the sign and try to guess the word that the sign means.

Many (but not all) sign language signs are iconic in nature, meaning they look like the actual object. Players may be able to guess or make really close guesses just by watching the movement of the hands and seeing what shape the hands are making, what the hands look like, etc. If you are playing this game with teens, you may want to make the game more complicated by having the leader sign a short sentence, for example *I go* (to the) *store.*

## Sign Language Picture Books

**Age Group:** upper elementary, 'tweens, teens

**Estimated Time:** three to five 1-hour sessions (depending on the age group/ability level)

**Materials Needed:** bound paper in the form of a book (you can find blank books made specifically for children to create their own books available for purchase; these may be sturdier and hold up longer than just a paper book); markers or crayons; magazines that participants may cut pictures out of, or a computer to allow them to print pictures that they want to use in their books; a camera; glue/paste; scissors

**Directions:** Let the participants of this program create an ASL picture book for your younger reading community and/or their parents. You could also use the books in your signing storytime programs if the theme is the same as your storytime theme.

First, have participants choose a theme that they'd like to use for their picture books, for example, mealtime signs, playground signs, action signs, playtime signs, etc. Any subject of interest may be used to create a picture book.

Second, participants should brainstorm the words they'll use in their books that support their theme. For example, if "playground" is chosen for the subject of the book, then include a slide, see saw, swings, etc. Once the words have been brainstormed, have everyone locate them in an ASL dictionary, preferably online so that they can see how the signs are made, to make sure that the words they chose are actual sign language signs. If not, some may be fingerspelled and therefore more difficult for small children to use, so they may want to limit themselves to just the words they can find signs for.

Third, have participants create the covers of their picture books and create one page for each word that they chose. If you're using bound books, then of course the number of words is limited to the number of pages in the book, as opposed to looseleaf notebooks, to which more pages could be added. The front is the cover, and on the back should be " About the Author" and "Summary," but all of the pages in between may be the words chosen. Have the children write the words very clearly, so that they will be easy for everyone to read. Once the books are laid out and completed, move on to step 4.

In this fourth step, cut out a picture of the word from a magazine or print one out from the computer. Glue the picture onto the appropriate page.

Fifth, after participants have determined the signs they'll be using and are working on the previous steps, pull them aside one by one to take photos of them making the signs. Once you have printed these out, give them to the participants to glue onto the appropriate pages in their books. Under each photo they should write a short description to explain how the sign is made.

Sixth, ask everyone to write a short summary of their books. They then need to do the "About the Author" section for the back cover.

Finally, have everyone check to make sure that they have a beautiful cover, with the subject heading and the author's name; that each page has a subject word, a picture of that word, a picture of the child making the sign, and a short description under the photo explaining how to make the sign; and that the back cover should have a short summary and about the author section. These books may then be put into circulation to be checked out and borrowed by families in your community, or you may show them to participants of your other sign language programs/storytimes. Some participants may really love their books and want to keep them. Leave it up to them whether they keep their books or allow others in the library to enjoy them. You may also offer your participants the opportunity to read and sign their books at your preschool storytimes.

### Open Mic—Poetry or Songs in Sign

**Age Group:** 'tweens, teens

**Estimated Time:** two 1-hour classes and one 2-hour open mic event

**Materials Needed:** poems or song lyrics, sign language dictionaries, room to hold an open mic evening event

**Directions:** Participants will be choosing a poem or song to sign along with and present at your library's "Open Mic Poetry/Songs in Sign Language" event. At your first meeting, have participants choose a poem or song that they'd like to learn how to sign along with. Have participants choose the keywords from each phrase or line to be signed and then look up those words in an ASL online dictionary so they can see on video how those signs are made and learn them.

At your second meeting, have the participants practice their song and poem and do a run-through of your open mic event. In ASL, words are often presented in a different order than in English. For example, the English-language question "Where is the baby?" is "Baby, where?" in ASL. However, when presenting a poem or song in English to hearing people and using ASL along with it, signs that match the English words may be shown at the same time that the word is said. For example, when signing the Pledge of Allegiance, signs are shown while saying the English words. It is important to have the participants sign only the keywords in the phrase or line; not every word in English exists in ASL.

If you want to sign the sentence, "I will go to the store," sign only "I go store". The sentence will still make sense and be understood by those who only sign, because you have chosen the keywords. There is something called Signed Exact English, in which one signs every single word in the sentence in English sentence order. However, we are not using Signed Exact English. Because we are trying to stay as true to ASL as we can, cut out the excess words and use actual ASL signs for your keywords.

A certified sign language teacher or interpreter can also help with this, so for accuracy purposes, you may want to invite a Certified American Sign Language Teacher or Certified Sign Language Interpreter to come to the second program meeting to help participants. They can ensure that the participants are using the right signs and making them correctly before they present them to an audience. This responsibility would then not fall on you when you are learning how to sign yourself.

Your third and final meeting will be an "Open Mic Poetry and Songs in Sign Language Event." It is open mic because it is great to invite the community to come and present a poem or song in sign language if they want to, and they will be good role models for the participants in your program. You may want to specifically invite deaf and/or hearing impaired students, high school or college ASL students or instructors, sign language teachers, and/or interpreters to come and share a poem or song with the rest of the audience as well as your program participants. Participants should say and sign their poems or songs simultaneously for the audience. Refreshments add a nice touch to this program.

### Create a Baby Sign Language Video

**Age Group:** 'tweens, teens

**Estimated Time:** 4–6 hours (may be separated into shorter blocks of time—three 2-hours sessions, for example)

**Materials Needed:** video camera, objects determined by the group, access to online ASL dictionary, video software or video online program access so that you can put video clips together to make a DVD.

**Directions:** Program attendees will create a video that you may put into circulation and/or show at a baby/toddler sign and rhyme storytime. At the first meeting, decide who is going to be responsible for which job, or participants may want to take turns at each job. You need a videographer, a prop person, and signers/performers.

Once you have decided whether you will rotate jobs throughout the video process or assign them, the group should decide on a theme for the video. What signs would they like to focus on? Food? Weather? Toys? After deciding on a theme, brainstorm words to show the signs for, as well as any nursery rhymes or songs that babies enjoy that fit into the theme. For example, if you do a nighttime theme you may want to include "Twinkle, Twinkle Little Star. "

Discuss what props you need to demonstrate the chosen words and start to gather them. From then on, you will work on your video. In the video, show the object and say the word. Show a few different people signing the word and then show the object again (maybe in a different way). For example, if you are doing a theme on toys and want to demonstrate the word ball, have a few different kinds of balls to show. Have the videographer take a video of the ball and someone saying the word ball, then show a few signers signing the word ball while also saying it. Finally, show two people throwing a ball back and forth and then again show a ball, and add someone saying the word "ball."

Move onto the next word. Keep doing this until you have videotaped all of the words that your program participants have decided to use. You may want to include a song, nursery rhyme, or short story in sign language in between video segments to make the video more interesting. These of course will have to be learned in sign language by the signers in the video before they are videotaped demonstrating them.

Once you are finished with videotaping, put the video clip segments together to make one DVD. When you are done, you'll have a DVD on a certain theme or topic that presents words in ASL and that can be used by families with babies and preschoolers. If you are going to use this video in any public viewings, you will need releases from the participants, or from their parents/guardians if they are under 18.

### Kids Helping Kids

**Age Group:** 'tweens, teens

**Estimated Time:** 2 hours (1 for preparation and 1 for participation)

**Materials Needed:** whatever materials you will be using in your preschool storytime

**Directions:** Have participants come to your library to work with you on planning your next signing storytime theme. First, choose one or two activities that the participant will sign for the preschool children. For example, if you choose a book to read, the participant may show the preschoolers the signs you are using to support the book, and may sign along with them as the story is read.

Second, teach the participant the signs he or she will need to know to participate in those chosen storytime activities (use the online dictionaries to look up any sign you don't already know). Have them practice the signs and also practice signing along with the activity as you practice conducting it.

Third, participants attend your signing storytime and help you show the preschool children the ASL signs.

Libraries that offer programs incorporating ASL for 'tweens and teens not only have the opportunity to offer fun and different programs, but they also help hearing children become more aware of the hearing impaired and deaf community. They will be learning better how to interact and communicate with those with special needs and will learn to be more accepting of other people and children with differences. Participants in your program will have a great time learning something new and at the same time how to be accepting and helpful community members.

# Chapter 13

# Final Thoughts

All the program ideas that you have read about in this book are intended to help you and your community learn more about American Sign Language and how it is used. They are meant to help you invite hearing impaired children into your library and help them to feel more comfortable interacting with hearing children while in the library. They are also intended to help teach your community members to be accepting of others who may be different in some way from the "norm." Last but not least, they are meant to be fun, an added element of fun for your existing library programs and for new programs that you might have never done before that will be very interesting to your library community.

Most important, have fun including sign language in your programs and learning some new signs. Enjoy the programs suggested in this book and pick one or two that you think you and your library community would really enjoy, then give them a try. You'll find not only that sign language is educational and provides numerous benefits, but that you've also added a new element of fun to your library and the programs that it presents. The feedback you'll get from community members will be similar. Enjoy!

# References

Acredolo, L. P., and S. P. Goodwyn. 2000. The long-term impact of symbolic gesturing during infancy on IQ at age 8. Paper presented at the meetings of the International Society for Infant Studies, Brighton, UK, July. Available at https://www.babysigns.com/index.cfm?id=64. Accessed January 21, 2010.

Daniels, Dr. Marilyn. 2001. *Dancing with Words: Signing for Hearing Children's Literacy.* Westport, CT: Bergin & Garvey.

Ernst, Linda. 1995. *Lapsit Services for the Very Young: A How-to-Do-It Manual.* New York: Neal-Schuman.

Everything Preschool—Early Childhood Education Made Easy. n.d. Available at http://www.everythingpreschool.com/. Accessed January 21, 2010.

Garcia, Joseph. 2002. *Sign with Your Baby: How to Communicate with Infants Before They Can Speak.* rev. ed. Seattle, WA: Northlight Communications.

Preschool Education—Discover the Fun in Learning. 1997–2009. Available at http://www.preschooleducation.com/. Accessed January 21, 2010.

Principles of Teaching. 2005. Available at http://teacherworld.com/potdale.html. Accessed September 28, 2010.

# Glossary of Signs

Here is a complete list of all of the signs that have been used in the programs suggested in this book, as well as their accompanying photo. Although the photographs give you a good indication of how to create each sign, sign language is three-dimensional, and many signs require movement. This glossary of signs explains in more detail how to implement each sign suggested.

**A**

**Again**—Bent hand's fingers touch palm of other hand.

**All Done (Finished)**—Hands start facing yourself, then flick them outward.

**All gone**—Pull open fingers across your palm as you close them into a fist.

**Animals**—Bent hands near armpits and wave your arms forward and back.

**Apple**—Knuckle of your pointer finger twists in your cheek.

**Asleep (Sleep)—Hand starts open and facing toward you as you close your fingers and pull down, closing your eyes and letting your head fall as if you're going to sleep.**

**B**

**Baby—Lay your arm on top of your other one and rock back and forth (as if rocking your baby).**

**Bananas—Pointer finger stands up (the banana) while the other pulls down as if peeling it.**

**Bath—Rub your fists up and down as if washing yourself.**

**Bathroom—The manual letter T waves back and forth (from the elbow, not twisting from the wrist).**

**B**

**E**

**Beans—Fingerspell B E A N.**

**A**

**N**

**Bear—Clawed hands scratch at the front of your shoulders.**

**Bed—Lay your head down on your hands.**

**Bee—The manual letter F touches your cheek, then make your hand flat and swat it away.**

**Big—Hands move apart to show the size.**

**Black—Pointer finger pulls across your forehead.**

**Blanket—Hands hold a blanket and pull it up to your shoulders.**

**Blueberries—Blue (twist the manual letter B) + berries (Hold your pinky finger with all of your other fingers and twist back and forth.)**

Blue—Twist the manual letter **B** back and forth.

Book—Hands together open and close.

Boy—Hand starts open and closes down as if grabbing your baseball cap.

Bread—Bent hand slices back of other hand..

Break—Hold "it" in your hands with fists and pull both hands down as if breaking it.

Brown—The manual letter **B** pulls down the side of your face.

Brush—Hand in a fist with thumb to the side moving back and forth as if brushing your hair.

Brush teeth—Pointer finger moves back and forth in front of your mouth, as if brushing your teeth.

Bubble(s)—Open and close your index finger and thumb with both hands, making the bubbles in different spots in front of you.

Bunny—Two fingers of both hands face backward on your head (making bunny ears).

C

Cake—Pull slightly bent **C** shape hand across the palm of your other hand (showing a slice of cake).

Carrot—Fist up near your mouth inches closer and closer to your mouth as you chomp.

Cat—Open hand with index finger and thumb opening and closing on your cheek as if feeling your cat whiskers.

Cereal—Bend your index finger up and down from your knuckle as you pull it across your chin.

Chair—Two fingers tap your other two fingers twice. If you lay them down and leave them there, that is the sign for "sit."

Cheese—Flat hands twist back and forth on each other as if squishing the cheese in your hand.

Clean—Flat hand pulls across other flat hand.

Chicken—Sign "bird" with your index finger and thumb opening and closing by your mouth making the bird's beak, then make your index finger peck on the palm of your other hand

Close eyes—Index finger and thumb start open and then close by your eyes.

Cold—Both hands in fists shake back and forth.

Color—Wiggle your fingers on your chin.

Come back—Both index fingers start pointing away from you and then pull toward you

Cookies—Claw shape hand presses down on other palm (like a cookie cutter).

Corn—Clawed hands twist forward and back (as if holding and eating corn on the cob).

Cow—Thumb on your head with your pinky finger sticking up.

Crow(s)—Fingerspell C R O W.

Crackers—Fist knocks on your other elbow.

D

Dad/Daddy—Thumb of your open hand taps on your forehead.

Day—Rest elbow on your other hand, index finger falls down until all lying completely down on other arm.

Diamond—Manual letter D taps on your ring finger.

Dirty—Rest hand under your chin and wiggle your fingers.

Dinner—Eat (closed hand taps mouth) + night (bent hand goes over your other wrist).

Dog(s)s—Pat your leg and then snap.

Donkey—Thumb on your head, flap the other four fingers forward and back.

Down—Point down with your index finger.

Dream—Index finger starts by touching your forehead, then wiggle finger as you pull it away.

Drink—Thumb lies just under your mouth, tilt hand up as if taking a drink out of a cup.

Dry—Pull bent index finger across your chin.

Duck/Ducky—Two fingers close down onto your thumb by your mouth.

E

Eat—Closed hand taps mouth.

Eight—Middle finger touches thumb.

Elephant—Flat hand comes out from nose, showing the elephant's trunk.

Everyone—Every (thumbs up on each hand, one hand brushes down behind the other) + 1 (index finger shows the number 1).

Excuse Me—Bent fingers move across palm, then point to yourself.

F

**Fall (down)—Two fingers start standing on your palm, then fall down.**

**Farm—Thumb of open hand brushes across chin.**

**Fish—Wiggle flat hand back and forth as it moves across in front of you.**

**Farmer—Farm (thumb of open hand brushes across chin) + person (flat hands in front of you move down).**

**Five—Four fingers and thumb up facing you.**

**Food—Same sign as eat, closed hand taps mouth.**

**Four—Four fingers up facing you.**

**Friday—Manual letter F faces you and moves in small circles.**

**Friend(s)—Index fingers link one way and then the other.**

**Friendly—Wiggle the fingers of your open hands on each side of your face.**

**Frog—Two fingers jump out from under your chin.**

**Fruit—Manual letter F twists by the corner of your mouth.**

**G**

**Geese—Fingerspell, or open and close all fingers onto your thumb (like bird but with all fingers instead of just the index finger)**

**Girl—Thumb brushes your jawline as it comes forward.**

**Glad/Happy—Brush flat hand(s) upward on your chest.**

**Goat—Fist knocks chin, then two fingers stick up from forehead (hand facing you).**

**Gold**—Point to your earring, then shake the manual letter Y down twice.

**Good**—Flat hand starts at chin and lands down on your other hand.

**Good-bye**—Like the gesture waving good-bye.

**Grapes**—Clawed hand taps as it moves up your forearm.

**Gray**—Fingers of open hands brush back and forth through each other.

**Green**—Manual letter G twists.

**H**

**Hello**—Flat hand starts at forehead and comes forward.

**Help**—Fist with thumb up rests on other flat hand and they both come upward together.

Hen—Fingerspell H E N

Hide—Fist with thumb lying on top goes under your other flat hand (as if hiding).

Hog—Fingerspell or sign pig (flat hand rests under your chin, fingers move up and down).

Horn—Hands near your mouth, wiggle fingers as if playing a horn.

Horse—Thumb on head, two fingers flap up and down.

Hot—Clawed hand facing your mouth flicks forward.

Hot dog—Index finger taps chin and then taps your palm twice (representing a hot dog in a bun).

**How**—Two hands in fists facing each other with thumbs on top, one hand twists forward and back.

**Hug**—Lay hands on your upper arms as if giving yourself a hug.

**Hungry**—Hand in the manual letter C pulls down your body.

**Hurt**—Two index fingers push toward and away from each other.

**I (the letter)**—Pinky finger facing out.

**I (me)**—Point to yourself.

**I love you**—Thumb, index, and pinky fingers.

**Ice cream**—Fist moves up and down near mouth, as if licking an ice cream cone.

**In**—Fingers closed on thumb go inside other cupped hand.

**J**

**Juice—Draw the letter j with your pinky finger.**

**K**

**Kiss—Fingers touching thumb tap on cheek (as if giving kisses).**

**L**

**Library—The manual letter L moves in circles outward.**

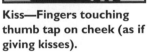

**Light—Flick the bottom of your chin with your middle finger.**

**Lights off—Open hand closes.**

**Lights on—Closed hand opens.**

Like—Pull open hand away from you as your middle finger and thumb meet.

Love—Fists in a cross on your chest.

Lunch—Eat (closed hand taps mouth) + noon (elbow rests on hand, top hand is flat).

M

Magic—Wiggle your fingers as both hands come forward.

Meat—Thumb and index finger hold the meaty part of your hand between your index finger and thumb of other hand.

Meet—Two index fingers come toward each other.

Melon—Flick middle finger on back of other flat hand.

Milk—Open and close your fingers.

**Mine/My—Lay flat hand on your chest.**

**Mom/Mommy—Thumb of your open hand taps on your chin.**

**Monday—The manual letter M faces you and moves in small circles.**

**Moon—Make a crescent shape with your index finger and thumb, start near your eye and move upward toward the sky.**

**More—Tap fingertips of both hands.**

**Morning—Flat hand lies on top of your arm (near elbow) and your bottom hand comes up toward you (also with a flat hand).**

**Moth—Fingerspell M O T H.**

**Mother—Thumb of your open hand taps on your chin.**

**Mouse—Index finger brushes across your nose.**

**My—Lay flat hand on your chest.**

**My turn—Thumb and index finger lie on your chest.**

**N**

**Name—Two fingers of one hand, tap on the two fingers from the other hand.**

**Nice—Brush flat hand across the other flat hand.**

**Night—Bent hand goes over the other arm at the wrist (like the sun going down over the horizon).**

**Nine—Index finger on the thumb.**

No—Two fingers snap down onto the thumb.

None (no, as in no more left)—both hands make an O.

O

Off—Start with one hand lying on top of the other one, then lift the top hand off.

On—One hand lies on top of the other.

One—Hold up the index finger.

Orange—Open and close your fist below your chin (like squeezing juice out of an orange).

Our(s)—Hand moves from one shoulder (one closest to the arm you're signing with) to the other one.

Out—Fingers begin inside your cupped other hand and then come out.

**Owl—Hands shaped like Os twist back and forth over your eyes.**

**P**

**Peach—Claw hand brushes your cheek and closes as it pulls away from your face.**

**Pajamas—Sign P J.**

**Pear—Wrap fingertips around other hand and pull away from it.**

**Peas—Tap your fingertip up your index finger.**

**Pig—Flap your fingers up and down under your chin.**

**Pillow—Hold your hands like you're holding a pillow under your head and push your hands in and out as if fluffing it.**

Pink—Manual letter P, middle finger brushes down your chin.

Pizza—Two fingers out draw the letter Z.

Play—Thumbs and pinky fingers out, twist both hands a few times.

Please—Rub flat hand on your chest.

Popcorn—Index fingers take turns popping up.

Purple—Shake the manual letter P back and forth.

Plum—Fingerspell P L U M.

Q

R

Rabbit—Two fingers of both hands up on your head making rabbit ears.

Rainbow—Four fingers out on both hands, the top hand draws a rainbow up toward the sky.

Red—Index finger starts at your lips and brushes down your chin.

Rooster—Thumb on your forehead with two fingers sticking up.

S

Salad—Both hands open move up and down as if tossing a salad.

Saturday—Manual letter S faces you and moves in small circles.

**See**—Two fingers up, middle one touches under your eye and hand moves forward a little bit.

**See you**—Just like see but hand moves toward the other person.

**Seven**—Ring finger touches the thumb.

**Share**—Both hands are flat with thumb up, top hand brushes forward and back.

**Sheep**—Two fingers act like scissors opening and closing as they move up your arm.

**Side**—One flat hand moves down the side of your body.

**Sign**—Index fingers of both hands rotate in circles toward the body.

**Silver**—Point to your earlobe and then shake the manual letter S down twice.

**Six**—Pinky finger touches the thumb.

**Sky—Hand moves across in an arc in front of you, showing the sky above.**

**Sleep—Open hand closes near your chin as it goes down your face, eyes close and head to the side.**

**Snake—Two fingers slither out from your chin.**

**Soap—Fingers rub in circles on palm of other hand.**

**Song—Flat hand moves back and forth above your other forearm.**

**Sorry—Manual letter S rubs in circles on your chest.**

**Soup—Two fingers come up from your palm toward your mouth.**

**Spaghetti—Pinky fingers start touching and make small circles forward as they move away from each other.**

**Squirrel—Knuckles of your top hand tap the knuckles of your bottom hand a few times.**

**Stand—Two fingers "stand" on your palm.**

**Star—Index fingers take turns pointing up to the sky while they remain side by side.**

**Stay—Pinky and thumb out, hand moves down in front of you.**

**Story—Open hands close as they touch each other, then twist and repeat.**

**Storytime—Story (open hands close as they touch each other, then twist and repeat) + time (index finger touches the top of your wrist).**

**Strawberries—Manual letter F comes forward out from corner of your mouth.**

**Sunday—Flat hands make small circles outward.**

**Sun/Sunny—Draw a circle in the air with your index finger, then open your hands to show the rays of the sun coming down.**

T

Take turns—Index finger and thumb out toward you and then toward me.

Ten—Thumb up shakes back and forth.

Thank you—Flat hand comes forward from chin.

There—Index finger points.

Thirsty—Index finger brushes down your neck.

This—Index finger points down in front of you.

Three—Two fingers and the thumb.

Thursday—Manual letter T and then H face you and move in small circles.

**Time—Index finger touches the top of your wrist.**

**Tired—Bent hands near armpits, arms droop down along with your shoulders and head.**

**Today—Pinkies and thumbs out and facing up, bounce hands twice.**

**Together—Fists together, thumbs facing up, move them around in a circle.**

**True—Index finger moves forward from mouth.**

**Tuesday—Manual letter T faces you and moves in small circles.**

**Tub—Fingerspell T U B.**

**Tummy hurts—Index fingers move toward and away from each other in front of your tummy.**

**Turkey—Index finger and thumb face down against chin and wiggle back and forth.**

**Twinkle—Use the sign for shine, middle fingers wiggle as you move hands up and away from each other.**

**Two—Two fingers up facing you.**

**U**

**Up—Index finger points up.**

**Up above—One hand rises above the other.**

**V**

**Vegetable—Manual letter V twists at the side of your mouth.**

W

**Warm**—Hand opens as it comes away from your mouth.

**Wash**—Fist (with thumbs on the side) rubs in circles on top of other fist.

**Washcloth**—Flat hands rub in circles in front of your face, then with index fingers draw a square.

**Water**—Manual letter W taps on your chin.

**Wednesday**—Manual letter W faces you and moves in small circles.

**Watermelon**—Water (manual letter W taps on your chin) + melon (middle finger flicks top of your other fist).

**Where**—Index finger moves back and forth.

Wet/Water—Hands gently open and close as they move up and down.

White—Open hand closes as it pulls away from your chest.

Who—Thumb on chin, pointer finger bends up and down.

Wind—Both hands open move from right to left as if pushing the air.

Winter—Hands in fists shake as if you're cold.

Wonder—Index finger makes circles near your forehead.

World—Both hands make the manual letter W, stack them, then the top hand moves forward, down and back around to land back up on top.

X

Y

Yellow—Pinky and thumb out, wiggle.

Yes—Fist nods up and down.

You—Index finger points to the other person.

Your(s)—Flat hand pushes toward the other person.

Z—Draw the letter Z with your index finger.

# Manual Alphabet

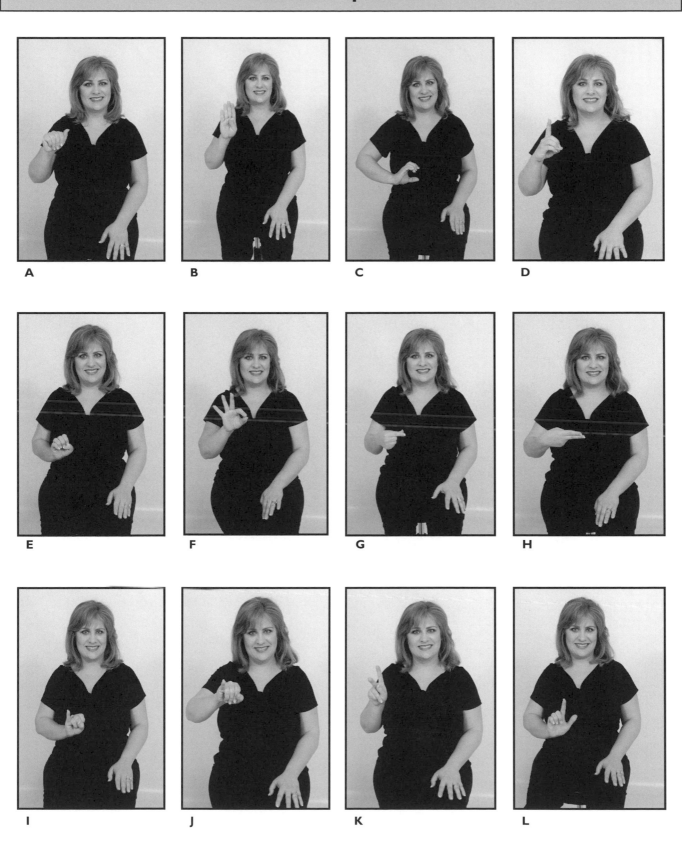

From *Once Upon a Sign: Using American Sign Language to Engage, Entertain, and Teach All Children* by Kim Taylor-DiLeva.
Santa Barbara, CA: Libraries Unlimited. Copyright © 2011.

# Manual Alphabet

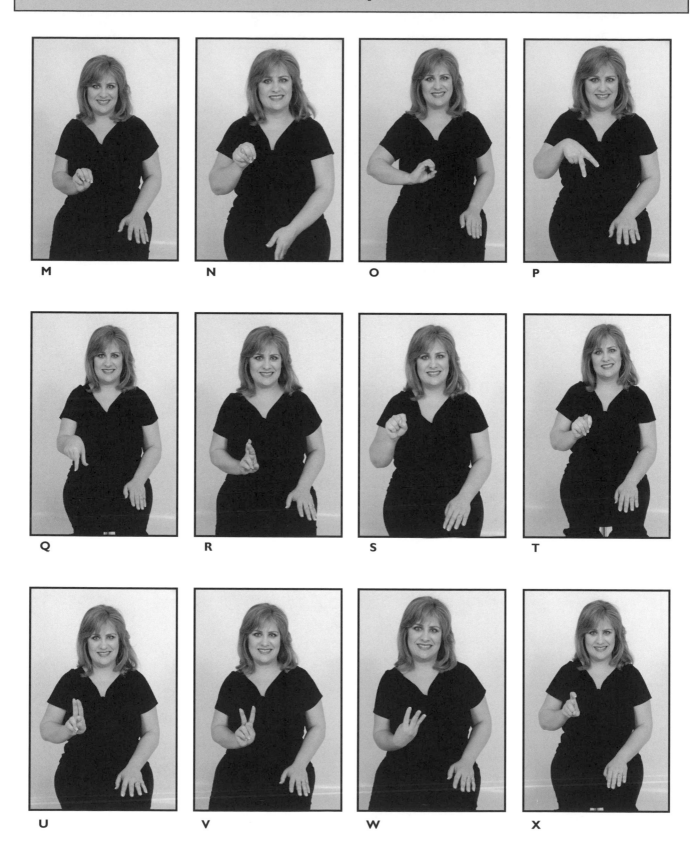

# Manual Alphabet

Y

Z

**Bathtub Template for Handprint Bathtub craft activity from Chapter 4**

**Moon and Star Template for Find the Stars and Moons craft activity from Chapter 5**

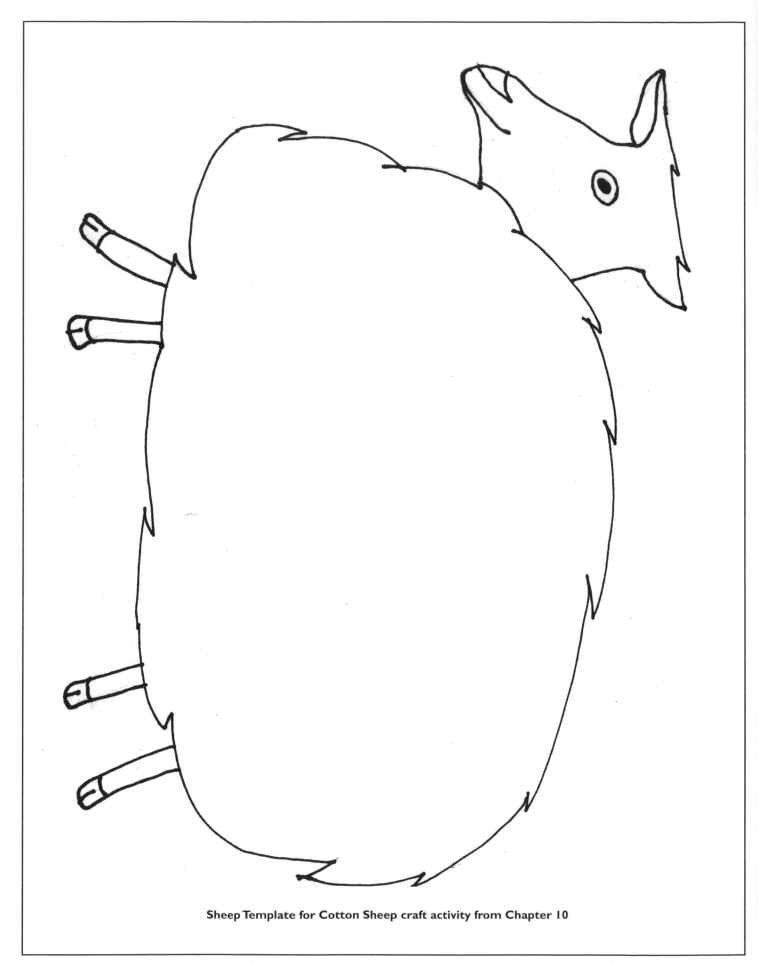

**Sheep Template for Cotton Sheep craft activity from Chapter 10**

## Books and DVDs

### Recommended Books for Adults

Bahan, Ben, and Joe Dannis. *Signs for Me: Basic Sign Language Vocabulary for Children, Parents & Teachers.* San Diego, CA: DawnSign Press, 1990.

Briant, Monta Z. *Baby Sign Language Basics: Early Communication for Hearing Babies and Toddlers.* New York: Hay House, 2004.

Briant, Monta Z. *Sign, Sing and Play: Fun Signing Activities for You and Your Baby.* New York: Hay House, 2006.

Butterworth, Rod. R., and Mickey Flodin. *Signing Made Easy: A Complete Program for Learning and Using Sign Language in Everyday Life.* New York: Perigee Trade, 1989.

Costello, Elaine. *Random House Webster's Concise American Sign Language Dictionary.* New York: Bantam Dell Publishing, 2002.

Costello, Elaine. *Random House Webster's Pocket American Sign Language Dictionary.* New York: Random House Reference, 2008.

Dennis, Kirsten, and Tressa Azpiri. *Sign to Learn: American Sign Language in the Early Childhood Classroom.* St. Paul, MN: Redleaf Press, 2005.

Duke, Irene. *The Everything Sign Language Book: American Sign Language Made Easy.* 2nd ed. Avon, MA: Adams Media, 2009.

Grayson, Gabriel. *Talking with Your Hands, Listening with Your Eyes: A Complete Photographic Guide to American Sign Language.* Garden City Park, NY: Square One Publishers, 2003.

Murray, Carol Garboden. *Simple Signing with Young Children: A Guide for Infant, Toddler, and Preschool Teachers.* Beltsville, MD: Gryphon House, 2007.

Sternberg, Martin L. A. *American Sign Language Dictionary.* 3rd ed. New York: Harper Perennial, 1998.

Tennant, Richard A., and Marianne Gluszak Brown. *American Sign Language Handshape Dictionary.* Washington, DC: Gallaudet University Press, 1998.

Valli, Clayton, ed. *The Gallaudet Dictionary of American Sign Language.* Washington, DC: Gallaudet University Press, 2006.

## Recommended Books for Children

Beginning Sign Language (Series). Eugene, OR: Garlic Press.

Breindel, Tina Jo, and Michael Carter. ASL Babies (Series). San Diego, CA: Dawn Sign Press.

de Azevedo Coleman, Rachel, and Emilie de Azevedo Brown. Signing Time (Board Book Series). Midvale, UT: Two Little Hands Productions.

Early Sign Langauge (Board Book Series). Eugene, OR: Garlic Press.

Fain, Kathleen. *Handsigns: A Sign Language Alphabet.* San Francisco, CA: Chronicle Books, 1993.

Flodin, Mickey. *Signing Is Fun.* New York: Perigee Trade, 1995.

Heller, Lora. *Sign Language for Kids: A Fun & Easy Guide to American Sign Language.* New York: Sterling, 2004.

Kubler, Annie. Sign and Sign Along (Series). Child's Play International.

Lewis, Anthony. Sign About (Series). Child's Play International.

Rankin, Laura. *The Handmade Alphabet.* New York: Puffin, 1996.

Warner, Penny. *Learn to Sign the Fun Way! Let Your Fingers Do the Talking with Games, Puzzles and Activities in American Sign Language.* New York: Three Rivers Press, 2001.

## Recommended DVDs for Children

My Baby Can Talk (DVD Series). Baby Hands Productions.

Sign-A-Lot (DVD Series). Dir. Barbara Granoff, Lee Sher.

Signing Time (DVD Series). Two Little Hands Productions.

We Sign (DVD Series). Production Associates.

## Online Resources

## Online Dictionaries for Adults

American Sign Language Browser—http://aslbrowser.commtechlab.msu.edu/

ASLpro.com—www.aslpro.com

ASL University—www.lifeprint.com

Baby Hands Productions—www.mybabycantalk.com

Handspeak—www.handspeak.com

Signing Savvy: Your Sign Language Resource—http://www.signingsavvy.com/

## Web Sites for Adults

ADCO Hearing Products, Inc.—www.adcohearing.com

Deafined: American Sign Language Education . . . One Sign at a Time—www.asldeafined.com/

Harris Communications—www.harriscomm.com

Lesson Tutor—www.lessontutor.com

R.I.T. National Technical Institute for the Deaf—www.ntid.rit.edu/dig/index.php

Signing Online: Providing Interactive Web-Based Instruction in American Sign Language—www.signingonline.com

## Online Dictionaries for Children

Baby Hands Productions—www.mybabycantalk.com

Born2Sign: Online Sign Dictionary—http://www.signwithme.com/002_browse_signs.asp

## Web Sites for Children

KiddiesSigns.com—http://www.kiddiesgames.com/en/sign_language_games.php

PBS Kids Arthur Sign Design—www.pbskids.org/arthur/print/signdesign

Signing Time! Kids—http://www.signingtimekids.org/

Starfall.com: Where Children Have Fun Learning to Read—www.starfall.com

## Recommended Baby Sign Language Classes

Sign2Me—http://sign2me.com

WeeHands—www.weehands.com

From *Once Upon a Sign: Using American Sign Language to Engage, Entertain, and Teach All Children* by Kim Taylor-DiLeva. Santa Barbara, CA: Libraries Unlimited. Copyright © 2011.

# Index

# About the Author

KIM TAYLOR-DILEVA is the owner of Kim's Signing Solutions (www.kimssigningsolutions.com), where she is an educational trainer on the benefits of using American Sign Language with hearing children. She has also developed several products to help parents and teachers use sign language at home and in the classroom. Prior to starting her business, she was an elementary school librarian and classroom teacher for more than 10 years.